Exam Grade B

GCSE French

Liam Porritt

Checked and approved by:	
Lindsay McDonald	Head of Modern Languages, Tonbridge School MA in Modern Languages (French & German), St Edmund Hall, University of Oxford
Esther Saurel	Head of French, Tonbridge School & native speaker L ès L (French), MFLE, Université Michel de Montaigne
Thérèse Coomber	Examiner for two international exam boards French teacher & native speaker L ès L, Université de Lille
Laurence Bass-Gualbert	French teacher & native speaker MA, Aix-en-Provence
Lionel Austin	Examiner for numerous exam boards Previous Head of Modern Languages, Tonbridge School & French teacher for over 30 years
Béatrice Austin	Examiner for two international exam boards French teacher & native speaker

Published by Exam Grade Booster
(Publisher prefix 978-0-9930429)
www.examgradebooster.co.uk
Second Edition published 2014

ISBN-13:   978-0-9930429-0-4

Disclaimer

The author and named checkers and approvers of this publication give no guarantee of improved examination performance nor will they be held responsible for any mistakes which may appear in this publication. They are not responsible if this publication, in any way, has a detrimental effect on its reader(s) or any other persons. This publication offers suggestions which have produced results for the author, but does not in any way state that these methods are the only ways of succeeding in GCSE or IGCSE examinations. All of the information given may not be entirely correct for all examination boards. The information given will not be inclusive of everything required for every examination board.

OTHER BOOKS BY THIS AUTHOR

Exam Grade Booster: GCSE Spanish

Exam Grade Booster: GCSE German

Exam Grade Booster: IGCSE Chemistry Edexcel

The Rules of Revision

OTHER BOOKS IN THIS SERIES

Exam Grade Booster: GCSE English

Exam Grade Booster: IGCSE Biology Edexcel

Exam Grade Booster: IGCSE Physics Edexcel

Contents

About Us

About The Author

I have been extremely fortunate to attend one of the best schools in the country and in this book I aim to share the outstanding, exam-focused teaching which has led to my success. I believe my experience and knowledge of revising for and then taking GCSE and IGCSE examinations make this guide uniquely suited to preparing any student for success in their own French exams.

It has taken me over two years to produce the second edition of this guide, having started it in the summer holiday following my GCSEs. The first edition received extremely positive reviews. The Independent Schools' Modern Languages Association called the book 'a very worthwhile purchase: wholeheartedly recommended' while one Amazon reviewer writes that the book 'has helped [her] immensely and [her] results are improving, with [her] confidence doing the same'. Therefore, I decided to keep a very similar format in this edition, with much of the same advice included, while also ensuring that I rectified issues raised by students who used the first edition. I firmly believe that this guide will enable any student, willing to spend a little time and effort, to boost their grade and make the most of their potential. My goal is to share with everyone the techniques and tricks I have learnt while studying French, particularly those which others can emulate in both the revision process and the exam room itself.

About The Checkers & Approvers

The checkers and approvers of this book are all qualified teaching professionals who, between them, have over 100 years of teaching experience. Four of the six are native French speakers and two have the invaluable knowledge of what it is like to learn French as an English speaker. They all share the author's goal of providing students in any schooling environment access to the same superb, exam-driven advice.

How to Use this Book

This book is designed to boost your French GCSE or IGCSE grade. It is suitable for both UK and International qualifications for all examination boards.

The book has three sections:

- The first section is designed to outline exactly what is required in each of the four parts of your French examination (writing, oral, reading and listening) in order for you to achieve better results.
- The second section will then target the areas of your French exam which you can improve using my tried and tested methods. It is essentially a tool box of things you need to boost your grade.
- The final part will give you specific essential learning to do. It contains the information you absolutely must know as well as clever hints and tips to help you understand the tricky bits.

The first section should be read through as you would read any ordinary book from start to finish. The second and third sections do not have any particular order, so I would advise you to flick through and pick out the areas you feel will be most useful.

There are some sections which are only applicable for either GCSE or IGCSE students, so skip over any bits which are not relevant to you. They are clearly marked.

Note: Throughout the book you will notice the appearance of the letter *e* in brackets, like so: (e). This signifies that if you are a girl, you must remember to add an *e* to the end of a word. If you are a boy, you must not put the *e*. You will also notice that there are some places where two different forms of a word are given (e.g. *fier / fière*) in which case the first form of the word is the masculine form and the second is the feminine form. This will generally only be given if the feminine form is irregular.

Section I

The Exam & What You Need To Do

Writing Examination

The writing examination is the **essay** component of the exam and will be marked according to the following three criteria:

1. **Communication**
2. **Use of language**
3. **Accuracy**

Communication

- Have you understood the assignment, and written appropriately (about the correct topic)?
- Do you respond to all the points of the assignment in your essay?
- Have you given opinions?
- Do you give justified reasons for the opinions given? E.g. why do you like or dislike something?
- Does your essay make sense?

If yes: you answer all the points clearly with reasons for why; and yes: the examiner can understand your essay, you will get **full marks** for this area.

So, how do you respond to all points of the assignment clearly?

Simple! All you have to do is write one paragraph for each point of the question. (I will explain more on this in a minute!)

The first and most crucial point about writing any essay in French is to make sure you write what you know, and don't write what you don't know. Do not be afraid to make up the content of your essay! The story of your essay does not have to be factually correct. The examiner does not know you and does not care if you have really done what you claim to have done. The exam is a test of your knowledge of the French language, not a test of how eventful your life has been. For example, if you went on holiday to Zimbabwe and ate wild crocodile and played the native African drums, don't try to say all that because you don't know how to... And neither are you expected to! You can make up **anything** as long as it answers all the points of the essay.

So how do you answer all the points of the essay?

Standard GCSE (not IGCSE)

Depending on your task, you will be given two, three or four points to answer in your writing assignment(s), and these will test:

- Your use of tenses: the past, present and future
- Your vocabulary

For example, if your assignment were as follows:

You went to visit a friend in France last year and you are writing an article about your stay. Don't forget to include what you liked and what you disliked about your visit. Also include how it was different from what you normally do on holiday.

The article should also include recommendations of what other people should do when they visit a friend in France, with reasons for these recommendations.

In the above assignment, you can use the following tenses:

Tenses	To...
Passé Composé and Imperfect (Past)	Describe what you liked and disliked about your stay
Present	Say what you normally do and how this particular holiday was different from that
Future and Conditional	Recommend things for people to do when they visit a friend in France

(If any of these tenses are not familiar to you, or you simply want to understand more about them, turn to pg. 76.) So, a minute ago I said that I would explain more on having one paragraph for each point of the question, and here it is: for the above assignment, to gain full marks for **Communication**, simply write three paragraphs. The first paragraph should be about what you liked and disliked about your stay, the second about what you normally do on holiday compared with what you did with your French friend, and the third should contain recommendations of what to do when visiting a friend in France. That's it.

IGCSE Only

You will be given four or five bullet points (in French) to respond to for each essay title and each of these will give you an opportunity to demonstrate your use of the various tenses and your knowledge of vocabulary.

For example, if the question were as follows:

You have spent a month working during the holidays. Write an article for a local newspaper about your experience. Mention:

- *Where you worked*
- *What the job involved you doing*
- *How much money you earned and how you normally spend your money*
- *Your opinion of the work*
- *Your plans for work this summer and why you would like to do this*

Note: The title and bullet points will both be in French.

Here, you could use the following tenses:

Tenses	To...
Passé Composé and Imperfect (Past)	Describe where you worked, what you had to do and how much money you earned
Present	Say what you normally spend your money on and your opinion of the work
Future and Conditional	Describe what you will do this summer for work and why you would like to do this

(If any of these tenses are not familiar to you, or you simply want to understand more about them, turn to pg. 76.) So, a minute ago I said that I would explain more on having one paragraph for each point of the question, and here it is: for the above question, to gain full marks for **Communication**, simply write five paragraphs with each one answering one bullet point. The first paragraph should be about where you worked, the second about what the job involved you doing, and so on...That's it.

 **All Candidates**

So, now you understand exactly how to structure your essay, you must understand the necessity for giving:

- Reasons why you did things
- Opinions of what you did
- Reasons for those opinions

If you want to get a high grade, this is not just important - it is **critical!** On every mark-scheme for every exam board there will be marks available for giving these three things, so make sure you give them all regularly throughout your essay. The French words *parce que* and *car* meaning *because* should appear at regular intervals throughout your essay... If they don't, it means you are not justifying your actions or opinions enough.

Use of language

This mark is awarded according to how well you use French. Do you know the basic and more complex tenses? Do you use fluid constructions, with justified opinions throughout your essay? Do you use long sentences with connecting words (such as *therefore*) to link ideas? (Don't worry; we'll come onto all this later.)

FIRSTLY, IT IS ESSENTIAL YOU USE A VARIETY OF TENSES THROUGHOUT YOUR ESSAY TO BOOST YOUR GRADE.

You should know the basic tenses (present, imperfect, *passé composé* and future) and if you don't, learn them ASAP (they are in the *Specific Essential Learning* section from pg. 80 to pg. 91). I know it's dull, but they are crucial. However, using set phrases, it is easy to spice up these tenses and you should already know some pretty simple but effective vocabulary which can be manipulated to form a good essay.

To boost your mark in this area, all you have to do is use your knowledge of tenses combined with set phrases. Use both the 'standard' phrases and the 'opinion' phrases in the correct places and use them to form long sentences which make sense – easy! (There is a list of both these types of phrase starting on pg. 35.) It is vital that you use both these types of phrase, as without opinion phrases you will not achieve a top grade – simple! Justifying why you do things throughout your essay is fundamental: always remember the three bullet points at the top of the previous page.

There is one more trick that will help to boost your **Use of language** mark: talking about other people. Throughout your essay you will spend most of the time talking about yourself, but to make it more interesting and to show off your grammar knowledge, try occasionally (maybe only twice) to mention someone else. For example, *Je voudrais travailler après l'école mais ma copine a l'intention d'aller à l'université.*

Accuracy

This is simply how few mistakes you make.

This is the hardest aspect to improve, and relies on your spelling, the correct use of tenses and agreement. This will be covered as fully as possible in the *Specific Essential Learning* section and also on pg. 54, which takes you through how to check your essays for grammar errors. However, if you learn the set phrases, and use them correctly, you can guarantee that they will be 100% correct, in both their use of vocabulary and tenses. Therefore, these phrases will improve your mark for both **Use of language** and **Accuracy**. I shall come onto **Accuracy** in more depth later, but in general:

> **GOLDEN RULE :**
> **WRITE WHAT YOU KNOW, DON'T WRITE WHAT YOU DON'T KNOW**
> Don't think of a sentence in English and then try to translate that into French because you will make mistakes. Instead, think what you know (phrases and vocab) and fit that into your essay.

I also have two other Golden Rules for your writing exam:

> ## GOLDEN RULE :
> ## DON'T WRITE TOO MUCH
> When you are given a word limit, don't go over it by too much because this will only increase the number of mistakes you make, and you will gain NO CREDIT for writing more.

> ## GOLDEN RULE :
> ## USE PHRASES BUT DON'T FORCE THEM
> When writing an essay, include as many phrases as you can, within reason. However, do not force them into an essay if they do not make sense. This will lower your **Communication** mark as well as your **Use of language** mark.

So, for more specific advice on your writing exam, including a list of brilliant phrases to boost your mark for **Use of language** and advice which will definitely improve your **Accuracy**, you should turn to pg. 34.

However, I would recommend you keep reading this section to find out how to boost your marks in your oral, reading and listening examinations, before turning to the *Tools to Boost Your Grade* section.

Standard GCSE (not IGCSE)

The section on your *Controlled Assessments* (starting on pg. 19) will give you more information on the writing component of your exam.

Oral Examination

....

Rules

Before the exam:

- Prepare answers to questions (related to your task if you are doing standard GCSE or related to topics on your syllabus for IGCSE) before the oral exam. The best marks for (I)GCSE orals will not necessarily be attained by the candidates who are best at speaking French, but instead by those who are best prepared. It is incredibly hard to come up with answers to questions spontaneously under the pressure of an exam. So, you must go through answers to questions before the exam itself. There is a list of virtually all possible questions for different topics on pg. 58.
- Prepare **opinions** and **reasons** for those opinions while you practice answering questions.
- In this preparation, use the same techniques as demonstrated previously in the *Writing Examination* section, using both standard phrases and opinion phrases to boost your mark (starting on pg. 35).
- It is up to you how you prepare. You can either write down answers to the oral questions or simply mentally prepare them. However, it is essential that you repeat your answers over and over again speaking them to yourself (over the course of a few weeks) so that, when it comes to the real exam, you have answered questions similar to the ones you are being asked before and therefore know roughly what to say.

Tip: Use your phone or tablet to record yourself speaking answers and then listen to your responses. This way, you will hopefully be able to spot some of the mistakes you make. Furthermore, the act of listening to yourself speaking is proven to help you remember information. So, answering questions will become easier the more you:

- Practise answering possible questions
- Listen to yourself

If there are words you find particularly difficult to pronounce, ask your teacher if he/she would mind you recording himself/herself saying these words for you to listen to and then say yourself.

- Make this preparation part of your routine as you do not need to be sat at a desk to do it! You could do it each evening, or while you are in the shower, or walking to school – whenever suits you, but make sure you do it.

IGCSE Only

You will have to do a short presentation, followed by a couple of minutes of conversation based on the topic you have chosen for your presentation. There will then be 2 more conversations of roughly 3 minutes, each of them broadly about 1 of the following topic areas: Home and abroad; Education and employment; House, home and daily routine; Modern world; Social activities, fitness and health. (There is a list of virtually every possible question for roughly these topics starting on pg. 58.)

As said above, it is up to you how you choose to prepare. However, I would advise preparing a few things which you can use for virtually any topic area:

- A description of a film. Say what it is about and why you liked it. This can be used if asked: What did you do on holiday? (*I went to see a film called... It was about...*) What did you do last weekend? What do you do in your free time? What did you do for your birthday last year?

Tip: It is quite hard to describe a film, so maybe look for a synopsis in French online, go through it with your teacher so that you understand everything, and then edit it so that it is not too long and it is in your own words. Add in your opinion of the film and reasons why you liked or disliked it at the end. (I am not encouraging plagiarism - that is wrong - but finding something online and then editing it to be your own is fine!) For my French oral, I used *Le Discours d'un Roi* (*The King's Speech*)... And notice I used the French title for the film as opposed to the English one; this is far more impressive.

- A description of a book. Say what it is about and why you liked it. (For my French oral I described and gave my opinion of *Le Da Vinci Code*.)

All Candidates

During the exam:

Sustain and expand on the answers you give. So, for example, the two following conversations are from two different candidates in their English oral:

Oral Conversation 1:
Examiner: "So, where do you normally go on holiday?"
Candidate 1: "I normally go to Spain."
Examiner: "Why do you go there?"
Candidate 1: "Because Spain is pretty and the weather is nice."
Examiner: "Where did you go last year?"
Candidate 1: "France."
Examiner: "Did you enjoy it?"
Candidate 1: "Yes."
Examiner: "So, where are you going to go next year?"
Candidate 1: "I am going to go to Spain with my family."
Examiner: "What are you going to do?"
Candidate 1: "Relax on the beach."
Examiner: "Anything else?"
Candidate 1: "Yeah, I'd like to read and would like to visit Barcelona."
Examiner: "Oh, how come?"
Candidate 1: "I'd love to see Gaudi's architecture."

Oral Conversation 2:
Examiner: "So, where do you normally go on holiday?"
Candidate 2: "I tend to go to Spain with my family because I think that it is very pretty and the weather is normally terrific. However, last year I decided to go to France with my friends and we had a great time because there were loads of things to do."
Examiner: "Where are you going to go next year?"
Candidate 2: "I am planning on going to Spain with my family, and I hope that the weather will be good because I would love to spend a week relaxing on the beach. I will spend lots of time reading and I will visit Barcelona because I've always dreamt of seeing Gaudi's architecture."

By which would you be more impressed? Well, Oral Conversation 2 would definitely score far more marks than the first one, **BUT** both these candidates know virtually the same amount of English (ok, the second knows slightly more vocab and a few neat phrases, but not that much more). So, the key here is to speak as much as possible. The questions from the examiner are there to prompt you as to what to say, not to trick you. You can tell how well your exam is going by how much the examiner speaks: the less the examiner speaks the better.

However, stay on topic. For the holiday example above, don't start talking about your school because this will lose you marks for **Communication**.

The key is to be prepared but, during the exam, to sound like what you are saying is completely spontaneous and that you are simply making it up as you go along (when of course you are not). This can be done by:

- Throwing in a few *umms* and *ahhhs*, to make it seem as if you are not just recalling a prepared answer, but actually speaking. This is essential!
- Trying to change your intonation (not ridiculously) throughout your conversation so that you don't sound like your most boring teacher.
- Not being embarrassed to try and use a French accent. There are marks on offer for your accent, and even if your accent is not brilliant, it is better than speaking French in a plain English accent. The examiner will be happy just because you are giving it a go. On the contrary, when you can't be bothered to even make an attempt at an accent and sound like a lost English tourist in Paris looking for 'Le Eiffel Tower' what impression do you think that gives?... First impressions count, so at least try.

So, the Golden Rules for your oral exam:

GOLDEN RULE :
SAY WHAT YOU KNOW, DON'T SAY WHAT YOU DON'T KNOW

GOLDEN RULE :
BE PREPARED BUT SOUND SPONTANEOUS

GOLDEN RULE :
EXPAND YOUR ANSWERS

GOLDEN RULE :
BREATHE SLOWLY AND REMEMBER: EVERYONE IS NERVOUS BEFORE THEIR ORAL!

Standard GCSE (not IGCSE)

Controlled Assessments: Writing & Oral Exams

You are lucky in comparison with people doing IGCSE. You are allowed to:

- Find out the precise title(s) of your essay(s) and oral conversation before your exam
- Plan your essay(s) and your oral in preparation for your exam
- Use a dictionary

The first thing to say is that the precise details of what you will have to do both in preparation for your tasks and in the tasks themselves will vary depending on which exam board your school uses for French GCSE. Most of you will have to write **two essays** and have **one oral conversation**. All three of these tasks need to be on **different topics**. The essays will each need to be around 250 words long. (However, you must confirm the exact details with your teacher.)

Writing

So, once you have found out the title(s) of your essay(s) (from now on I shall presume you will be writing two, but if not just adapt the system for one), you will need to stick to the following procedure in order to achieve the best possible marks.

| Find out essay titles | Write essays in own time | Produce plans and teacher feedback | Learn essays | Nail the exam! |

When writing your essays, you will be able to use:

- The material your teacher has given you on each of the topics covered in your two essays
- The material given in this book

This combination will help you to produce the best possible essays. They both need to be at the top end of the word limit, but remember not to go over it! All of the advice for the writing exam in the previous section applies here and is still crucial.

Once you have finished writing your essays, you need to produce a plan (the number of words allowed on this will depend on your exam board so ask your teacher) which you will be allowed to take into the exam room. Most exam boards also allow a few diagrams. It is up to you what you choose to write, but I would advise key words from each sentence which will prompt you what the rest of the sentence said along with a diagram which will remind you what each paragraph is about.

Note: Most exam boards will not allow you to include conjugated verbs in your plan, so you must put particular emphasis on learning exactly how the verbs you will be using in your essays (and your oral) conjugate.

For example, if one of my sentences were:

J'aime bien aller au cinéma avec mes amis parce que je peux m'échapper du monde réel. – I really like to go to the cinema with my friends because I can escape the real world.

I would include the following words in my plan:

cinéma, amis, s'échapper

Once you have completed your two essays and your two plans, your teacher will check through your plans and it will be up to you to make sure you learn your essays thoroughly. Then, all you have to do is copy them out in the exam room from your memory (with your plans to help you) and you are sorted!

I know that this sounds like an awful lot of work, but it really does produce the results you are after. I cannot guarantee anything, but I managed to get 100% in my Italian GCSE after just 8 months of studying the language using this technique. Trust me, when you get that result, all of the hard work preparing is worth it!

The last point to make is on the use of dictionaries. At the start I said that being able to use a dictionary was lucky... It is, but only if you use it properly.

Dictionaries should only have **two** uses in the examination room:

1. To **check** the **spelling** of any words included in your prepared essay which you are not 100% sure of as you write it out.
2. Very occasionally if there is a word which you know was included in your essay in English, but which you can't quite remember in French.

GOLDEN RULE :
DO NOT USE A DICTIONARY IN THE EXAM TO LOOK UP WORDS WHICH WERE NOT INCLUDED IN YOUR PREPARED ESSAY

If you have followed my system, there will be no need for this. Just remember the following Golden Rule when you are preparing your essays and when you are writing them out in the exam room:

GOLDEN RULE :
WRITE WHAT YOU KNOW, DON'T WRITE WHAT YOU DON'T KNOW

You will make sure you do this by using the information in your notes and in this book while writing your essays initially, only using a dictionary (can be online) to look up the occasional word.

Oral

The oral exam is in fact very similar to the writing exam. You will know the precise topic area of your oral conversation before the exam itself, so (using the questions on pg. 58 and any information your teacher may give you) you need to prepare answers to questions which you could possibly be asked. Once you have done this – either mentally or writing them down – you need to become familiar with your answers so that you can use parts of what you have prepared in the exam itself.

That's all there is to it really. All of the previous advice for both the oral and writing exams still applies when you are preparing for and taking your controlled assessments, so make sure you follow it!

Reading Examination

This about reading tell you boost at GCSE with easy steps. Don't worry; I know this is not good English (in fact there are 10 words missing). The point is that you don't need every detail to understand something. In your reading examination, you are **NOT** expected to understand every word. It is a test of your comprehension as well as your knowledge of French, so **DO NOT PANIC!** Use the words you understand to work out what the passage is about, and use clues such as the title or the questions in response to the passage in order to deduce what is going on. Here is a sample passage, which could be a text from a French GCSE Paper. There are no questions, but there are notes on how to establish what the article is about.

Pourquoi est-ce que les jeunes consomment de l'alcool aujourd'hui?
lundi 9 septembre 2014

De nos jours, il est clair que l'alcool fait partie du passage à l'adolescence, période pleine de curiosité mais sans souci des conséquences. Cependant, il ne faut pas oublier que la consommation d'alcool apporte des risques… Mais malgré ces effets néfastes bien connus, les adolescents continuent à l'utiliser principalement comme mode d'évasion. Pourquoi?

Pour un jeune, Vincent Baudin, l'alcool lui permet de se rebeller contre la société et ses parents. Il nous a dit : « Je bois pour oublier mes difficultés. L'alcool me déstresse et, pour moi, le plus important c'est qu'il me donne la confiance suffisante pour aborder le sexe opposé. » Selon une étude récente sur la curiosité de ces effets, c'est l'influence du groupe qui provoque les habitudes de consommation.

De plus, les adolescents ne l'utilisent pas que pour tester leurs propres limites, mais aussi celles de leurs parents. Ils veulent voir la réaction de leurs parents et en même temps se sentir mûrs et indépendants, comme s'ils n'avaient besoin de personne. L'adolescent doit savoir pourquoi l'autre boit, il expérimente, essaie, a besoin de connaitre les effets de la substance qui les rend adulte. Au bout du compte, c'est la nature humaine d'être curieux… Ne blâmez pas vos enfants, ce n'est pas de leur faute.

Cependant, le problème est qu'ils aiment souvent le sentiment de liberté produit par l'alcool et par conséquent ils continuent à s'enivrer de plus en plus souvent. Dans ce cas, les jeunes ne deviennent pas forcément accros, mais ils boivent pour se faire plaisir.

Attention certains jeunes ayant une véritable souffrance peuvent développer une dépendance à l'alcool! Pour certains jeunes qui souffrent de troubles de l'anxiété, ou qui ont des problèmes familiaux ou des conduites antisociales, la consommation d'alcool est une solution à toutes leurs difficultés.

Key Points to look for in Reading Exam Questions

Title

The title will give you an instant idea of what the article is about. Here, the title is clearly a question, so we can be pretty certain the article will be answering that question. You should know that *jeunes* are *young people* - this is very basic vocabulary. We can then see that it is a question about young people consuming (*consomment*) alcohol (*alcool*). *Consomment*, if you didn't know what it was, looks pretty similar to *consume*, and even if you didn't spot this, what else could young people be doing with alcohol other than consuming / drinking it!?

English Words

The highlighting on the next page shows all the words which we can work out purely from knowing English. From this alone, we can deduce most of what is being said in the passage. (If you didn't have a clue the first time you read it through, read it again once you have finished this page, paying close attention to the highlighting.) I would advise doing this in your exam: whilst you are reading through the passage, highlight or underline any words which are obvious to you from your knowledge of English, even if you haven't ever seen them before in French.

Furthermore, use other languages (if you do them) to help you work out what words mean if you do not recognize them. E.g. If you do Spanish, *la playa* means *the beach*... therefore, you can work out what *la plage* means in French (*the beach*)!

Read Questions Then Text

Read the questions **before you read the text** as these will give you a clue as to the content of the passage. They will also make you aware of the information you need to look out for when you are reading the text. (I know there are no questions for the text above... I am trying to show that even with a hard text and no questions you can still get the gist of it!)

Pourquoi est-ce que les jeunes consomment d'alcool aujourd'hui?
lundi 9 septembre 2014

De nos jours, il est clair que l'alcool fait partie du passage à l'adolescence, période pleine de curiosité mais sans souci des conséquences. Cependant, il ne faut pas oublier que la consommation d'alcool apporte des risques… Mais malgré ces effets néfastes bien connus, les adolescents continuent à l'utiliser principalement comme mode d'évasion. Pourquoi?

Pour un jeune, Vincent Baudin, l'alcool lui permet de se rebeller contre la société et ses parents. Il nous a dit: « Je bois pour oublier mes difficultés. L'alcool me déstresse et, pour moi, le plus important c'est qu'il me donne la confiance suffisante pour aborder le sexe opposé. » Selon une étude récente sur la curiosité de ces effets, c'est l'influence du groupe qui provoque les habitudes de consommation.

De plus, les adolescents ne l'utilisent pas que pour tester leurs propres limites, mais aussi celles de leurs parents. Ils veulent voir la réaction de leurs parents et en même temps se sentir mûrs et indépendants, comme s'ils n'avaient besoin de personne. L'adolescent doit savoir pourquoi l'autre boit, il expérimente, essaie, a besoin de connaitre les effets de la substance qui les rend adulte. Au bout du compte, c'est la nature humaine d'être curieux… Ne blâmez pas vos enfants, ce n'est pas de leur faute.

Cependant, le problème est qu'ils aiment souvent le sentiment de liberté produit par l'alcool et par conséquent ils continuent à s'enivrer de plus en plus souvent. Dans ce cas, les jeunes ne deviennent pas forcément accros, mais ils boivent pour se faire plaisir.

Attention certains jeunes ayant une véritable souffrance peuvent développer une dépendance à l'alcool! Pour certains jeunes qui souffrent de troubles de l'anxiété, ou qui ont des problèmes familiaux ou des conduites antisociales, la consommation d'alcool est une solution à toutes leurs difficultés.

So, using what I have said, here is the general idea of each paragraph. You could work this out without me. (Honestly, I know the passage seems complicated, but when you spend time to think about it and use the three key points on pg. 24, it's really not too bad!)

Paragraph 1: We can see that alcohol is related in the passage to adolescence, a period of curiosity, and something about consequences. Alcohol brings risks yet adolescents continue to use it principally as a mode of evasion (a way of escaping). Then there is a question (meaning *why?*).

Paragraph 2: We are given the opinion of one young person, Vincent Baudin. Alcohol is said to permit him to rebel against (*contre* means *against* and could easily be worked out here) society and his parents. There are then some speech marks (« and » are used for speech marks in French), and he says that alcohol de-stresses him and then something about sufficient confidence for the opposite sex. Then it moves away from Vincent to say that group influence (peer pressure) provokes habits of consumption.

Paragraph 3: Adolescents use it to test limits. There is something about their parents and their reactions along with them being big and independent. They experiment and want to know the effects of this adult substance. It is human nature to be curious and there is something about blaming infants (children) and it (not) being their fault.

Paragraph 4: The problem is they have sentiments (feelings) of liberty produced by alcohol with the consequence that they continue (to drink it) for pleasure (*plaisir*).

Paragraph 5: Attention! Certain young people with (*ayant* in fact means *after*) true suffering develop a dependence on alcohol. Certain young people with anxious troubles, family problems and antisocial behaviour use the consumption of alcohol as a solution to difficulties.

Having understood all of this, you will definitely be in a very strong position to answer any questions. Just remember this golden rule:

> ### GOLDEN RULE :
> ## YOU WILL NOT UNDERSTAND EVERY WORD, BUT YOU DON'T NEED TO

So, up until now, this section has dealt with getting the gist of the hardest passages on the reading examination paper. However, you still have the task of answering the questions which accompany these passages. On all (I)GCSE examinations the majority of questions do not involve you writing in French, but instead include box ticking, English responses and multiple choice style questions. Clearly to answer these questions, all you have to do is understand what both the passage and the questions mean.

Having said this, **examiners will try to trick you...**

...Therefore, there will always be a few questions in both the reading and listening papers designed to do just that. Examiners trick students by giving them two pieces of information to answer a question, with the first piece of information either not the precise answer to the question or only a part of the information needed to get the right answer, so please be careful and look out for this! For example, if the text translated to:

Nowadays, children spend an average of 2 hours and 45 minutes watching TV, and that doesn't even include the half an hour they spend on the internet or playing video games...

And you had to tick one of the boxes below:

Every day, children are in front of a screen for...

- ☐ *Two hours and fifteen minutes*
- ☐ *Two hours and forty-five minutes*
- ☐ *Three hours and fifteen minutes*

...I can guarantee that around 60% of students would tick the second box because they saw this piece of information in the text and jumped to the immediate conclusion that this must be the answer, without paying attention or thinking about the second piece of information given. So, make sure you are part of the 40% of candidates who gets this type of question correct. Avoid falling into the examiners' traps every time and you will be taking a firm step towards boosting your grade.

Note: There are some more ways in which examiners will try to trick you (although these are more common in the listening paper) on pg. 33.

Writing Answers in French

There is, for most exam boards (you should check with your teacher whether your exam board requires you to do this), a question which involves you writing the answers in French. This section will give you the tools you need to make sure you are able do this.

This is supposed to be one of the most difficult tasks you have to complete in your entire (I)GCSE examination. If you can do this, you immediately put yourself into the top bracket of candidates. To be honest, it really isn't that hard if you know exactly what you have to do. The following system requires minimal French knowledge and will ensure you know the precise technique needed to gain as many marks as you possibly can.

Pourquoi est-ce que les jeunes consomment de l'alcool aujourd'hui?
lundi 9 septembre 2014

De nos jours, il est clair que l'alcool fait partie du passage à l'adolescence, période pleine de curiosité mais sans souci des conséquences. Cependant, il ne faut pas oublier que la consommation d'alcool apporte des risques… Mais malgré ces effets néfastes bien connus, les adolescents continuent à l'utiliser principalement comme mode d'évasion. Pourquoi?

Pour un jeune, Vincent Baudin, l'alcool lui permet de se rebeller contre la société et ses parents. Il nous a dit: « Je bois pour oublier mes difficultés. L'alcool me déstresse et, pour moi, le plus important c'est qu'il me donne la confiance suffisante pour aborder le sexe opposé. » Selon une étude récente sur la curiosité de ces effets, c'est l'influence du groupe qui provoque les habitudes de consommation.

We have already analysed the above text (here I have only included the first two paragraphs) to deduce its meaning. There were previously no questions to accompany the text. This should have proved to you that you can understand the **vast majority** of any (I)GCSE passage without many tools to help you. However - now that I've convinced you of that - I am going to give you a couple of questions which require answers from the text above, **in French**. (Ignore the highlighting and underlining for now.)

1) <u>Pendant les années d'adolescence</u>, même si les jeunes comprennent les risques de l'alcool, <u>quelle est la raison primaire pour leur consommation</u>? [1]

First of all we need to understand the question. In order to do this we use the same methods we used to get the gist of the whole article and look for French words which resemble English ones, and also consider what the question is likely to mean. I have highlighted the words which have obvious English meanings. Now, often questions will contain more information than you really need, so you must deduce which part of the question is really necessary. (I have underlined it for you.) We then need to look at the text (near to the beginning because the questions will always be in the order the answers appear in the passage) for the primary reason for the consumption of alcohol during adolescence. The answer to this is underlined in the first paragraph (on pg. 28).

Tip: We are only looking for one primary reason because the question only has one mark (indicated by [1]) available.

Once you have found all the information you need, the key to answering the question is to use a mixture of:

- Words from the text
- Words from the question
- Your own words

So, using the above highlighting, an answer which would gain the mark available for this question would be:

Les jeunes continuent à consommer de l'alcool comme mode d'évasion.

Note: Very often students are worried about 'lifting' (i.e. copying directly) from the text and so try to change everything into their own words and in the process lose marks. Examiners do not expect you to rephrase *comme mode d'évasion*, so don't try to. Instead, do simple things like using the verb *consommer* instead of the noun *la consommation*. There are no marks on offer for the quality of language used in your answers; they just need to make sense!

2) Selon l'article, qu'est-ce que Vincent Baudin a dit en ce qui concerne <u>le rapport entre le sexe opposé et la consommation d'alcool</u>?
[2]

If we do exactly the same as we did on the first question, we see that the question is essentially asking for what Vincent Baudin says about the opposite sex and the consumption of alcohol. The answer to this is again underlined in the text (on pg. 28).

> **Tip:** This time, we need to look for two details because the question is worth two marks (indicated by [2]).

Here we have an issue which we did not come across in the last question and which is incredibly common in (I)GCSE exams. We need to say what alcohol does to *Vincent Baudin*, but the article says what alcohol does to *me*, because it is Vincent Baudin who is speaking. If you 'lift' the answer directly from the text you will get **no marks** because you are talking about the influence of alcohol on *me* rather than its influence on *Vincent Baudin.* I cannot reiterate enough how important the skill of being able to change the information you are given in the text into the person required by the question is. This is so crucial that it is one of my Golden Rules. If you aren't good at this, ask your teacher to practice it with you.

GOLDEN RULE :
KNOW HOW TO MANIPULATE INFORMATION IN THE TEXT
It is crucial your answer makes sense, and if you get this wrong it can be incredibly costly!

So, my answer to this question would be:

La consommation d'alcool donne à Vincent Baudin la confiance suffisante pour aborder les filles.

Easier Reading Examination Questions

We have now addressed every aspect of the harder questions which will appear in your reading exam, but what about the easier ones? These easier questions are effectively a basic vocabulary test. You simply need to know the kinds of words they are likely to test you on and to learn these. There is a list of this kind of basic vocabulary which you absolutely must know starting on pg. 65. **These lists are by no means extensive vocab lists; you need to learn more than just these!** However, they do provide a brief accumulation of what I deem to be the most common, topic-specific words within all (I)GCSE syllabuses. Therefore, it is crucial that you learn these words properly and that you know them all by the time you take your exam. (There is also advice on how to learn vocabulary on pg. 63.)

Finally, make sure you obey the two following golden rules. Every year a handful of people drop down a grade or two by not following these rules, regardless of their ability. Please be careful and don't fall into these traps!

Advice contained in the *Listening Examination* section is also applicable here.

GOLDEN RULE :

ANSWER THE QUESTION IN THE RIGHT LANGUAGE

If the question asks for answers in English, make sure you give them in English. If it asks for them in French, give them in French! If you don't, you will lose all of the marks available for an entire question.

GOLDEN RULE :

GIVE THE INFORMATION YOU ARE ASKED TO GIVE

If the question asks you to tick 5 boxes, tick 5 boxes. If you have ticked 4 and are not sure of the last one, take a calculated guess. BUT, most importantly, do not tick 6! If you do you will probably lose all of the marks for that question.
Similarly, if you are asked: *What is Sammy's favourite toy?* make sure you do NOT write down what John's favourite toy is!

Listening Examination

All of the advice (particularly the Golden Rules) given in the previous *Reading Examination* and *Writing Answers in French* sections applies to the listening exam, so read from pg. 23 if you haven't already.

First of all, you must have read and understood all of the questions which will be answered in the passage you are about to listen to **before** the recording begins to play. You are given plenty of time at the start of the exam and in between passages, so make sure you know exactly what the questions are looking for **before** the passage even starts.

Tip: Underline key words in the questions **before** the passage starts to play. This way, you'll know what information you need to listen out for. Be aware that the passage will probably not use exactly the same word as in the question, so listen out for words with the same or a similar meaning.

But, be careful! Often questions will say something like:

1) Apart from hamburgers, what is Jimmy's favourite food?

It is not uncommon for examiners to see the answer *hamburgers*, because - as stupid as this may sound - some candidates are not careful enough or simply don't bother to read the questions before the start of the passage. Therefore, when they see *favourite food*, and hear the word *hamburgers*, they just write that down in the heat of the moment and quickly rush onto the next question. This is foolish and you cannot afford to throw away easy marks like this!

Once the passage begins to play - as obvious as this may sound - ensure you listen! Make sure you aren't too busy writing down an answer to hear the next part of the passage; it may contain the answer to the next question.

Solution: Write down, next to the answer space, either in English or French, a clear note or word, to remind you of the answer. You are given time at the end of each question and at the end of the exam to come back and change or insert any answers. It is better to have clues to the answers of all 5 parts of a question and get 3 correct, than to only hear 2 parts of the question, and so only score a maximum of 2 marks.

Make sure you listen out for words similar to English words and also for key words in the question. However, be wary that you may hear key words from the question, but the examiners are trying to catch you out using **negatives** and different **tenses**. Therefore, do not assume that the first word or phrase that you hear is the one you need for your answer. For example, if the question were:

2) How much pocket money does Tom receive each week?

… and you heard Tom say:

"Quand j'étais jeune, ma mère me donnait dix euros chaque semaine, mais maintenant elle me donne vingt euros chaque semaine."

… it would be easy to think that the answer you need is *10 euros*, because that is the first piece of information you are given which relates to the question. In fact, the answer is *20 euros*.

Similarly, if the question were:

3) How does Jenifer get to school?

… and the passage said the following:

"Jenifer ne va pas à l'école en voiture. Elle y va en train."

… many candidates would write that she goes by car, when in fact the answer is: *She goes by train*.

Finally, there is a list of crucial vocab for your listening exam starting on pg. 65 (they are the same lists as for the easy questions in the reading examination). **These lists are by no means extensive vocab lists; you need to learn more than just these.** However, at the start of the listening exam there will be a number of relatively easy sections where this vocab could come up, and if you want to succeed in the exam it is critical you score very well on these easier sections, so make sure you learn the vocab.

Section II

Tools To Boost Your Grade

Phrases

These phrases are organized into different categories for different time periods of your essay (i.e. past, present and future). You should have these pages open while you are writing any essay in French - at least for now. Remember that you need to show off your use of different tenses, so it is crucial that you use plenty of phrases from each time period over the course of your essay.

Although there are quite a few phrases here, when you have practised using them a couple of times, you should begin to familiarize yourself with the phrases you most like to use. Then, I would advise making your own list of your favourite ones, taking at least 3 phrases from each category. Learn these for your exams.

After that, use these phrases either while preparing for assignments (for standard GCSE) or during the examination itself (for IGCSE).

+ verb = followed by any verb
+ inf. = followed by the infinitive form
(e.g. to do = faire) of any verb
+ pa.p. = followed by a past participle
(e.g. done = fait)
+ pr.p. = followed by a present participle
(e.g. doing = faisant)
+ cond. = followed by conditional
(e.g. I would do = je ferais)
+ subj. = followed by subjunctive

+ noun = followed by any noun
+ adj. = followed by any adjective

Don't worry what these mean; you don't have to understand the terminology or why they are used. Just make sure that when you use a phrase, you also use the correct part of speech. (They are all in bold.)

Note: See pg. 45 for the *List of Useful...* section. This will give you lists of each of the parts of speech for you to use with these phrases.

Tip: Make sure you're careful of phrases ending in *de* or *que* because these need to change to *d'* or *qu'* when they are followed by a word which starts with a vowel. (E.g. Je pense **qu'il** est...)

Standard Phrases

Present

1) Je dois / peux / veux **+ inf.** – I have to (must) / am able to (can) / want to **+ inf.**

   Je dois / peux / veux **porter** un t-shirt blanc quand il y a du soleil. – I have / am able / want **to wear** a white T-shirt when it is sunny.

2) J'essaie de **+ inf.** – I try to **+ inf.**

   Quand je suis chez moi, j'essaie d'**aider** ma mère à faire les tâches ménagères. – When I am at home, I try **to help** my mum to do the chores.

3) Je pense que c'est / c'était **+ adj.** – I think that it is / it was **+ adj.**

4) Ça me fait plaisir de **+ inf.**… parce que… – I love to **+ inf.**… because…

   (3 & 4) Ça me fait plaisir de **nager** dans la mer parce que c'est génial pour la santé et je pense que c'est très **amusant**. – I love **to swim** in the sea because it is great for your health and I think that it is great **fun**.

5) J'ai envie de **+ inf.** – I feel like **+ pr.p.**

   J'aimerais aller au Canada parce que j'ai envie de **voir** un ours. – I would like to go to Canada because I feel like **seeing** a bear.

6) Je m'entends bien avec **+ noun** – I get on well with **+ noun**

   Je m'entends bien avec mon **frère**, mais je déteste ma sœur. – I get on well with my **brother**, but I hate my sister.

7) En **+ pr.p.** – On **+ pr.p.**

   En **arrivant**, nous avons décidé d'aller à la piscine. – On **arriving**, we decided to go to the pool.

8) Il y a **+ noun** – There is / are **+ noun**

   Il y a beaucoup de **choses** à faire là où j'habite. – There are lots of **things** to do where I live.

9) Il y a **+ time expression** – **Time expression** + ago

Note: Obviously this one would be followed by the past, even though it is technically a present expression!

Il y a **trois semaines**, j'ai joué au golf avec ma copine. – **Three weeks ago**, I played golf with my girlfriend.

10) Ça fait **+ time expression +** que **+ present verb** – I have been **+ pr.p. +** for **+ time expression**

Ça fait **dix ans** que **je joue** au rugby. – I have been **playing** rugby for **ten years**.

11) Bien que **+ subj.** – Although **+ verb**

Bien que **j'aie** le vertige, les montagnes russes étaient supers. – Although **I am** afraid of heights, the roller-coasters were awesome.

12) Je dois dire que... – I must say that...

i) Je dois dire qu'elle était la femme la plus sexy que j'aie jamais vue! – I must say that she was the sexiest woman I've ever seen!

ii) Je dois dire qu'il était l'homme le plus sexy que j'aie jamais vu! – I must say that he was the sexiest man I've ever seen!

13) Il y a un tas de **+ noun (plural)** – There are loads of **+ noun (plural)**

Il est important de dire qu'il y a un tas de **manières** de rester en forme. – It is important to say that there are loads of **ways** to keep fit.

14) Je me sens **+ adj.** – I feel **+ adj.**

15) Je suis en train de **+ inf.** – I am (in the process of) **+ pr.p.**

(14 & 15) Je me sens **fatigué(e)** quand je suis en train de **courir**. – I feel **tired** whilst I am (in the process of) **running**.

Note: Make sure you add an '*e*' to *fatigué* if you are a girl!

Past

Passé Composé

1) J'ai décidé de **+ inf.** – I decided to **+ inf.**

   J'ai décidé d'**acheter** des cartes postales parce que je voulais les envoyer à ma famille. – I decided **to buy** postcards because I wanted to send them to my family.

2) L'année dernière / La semaine dernière **+** je suis allé(e) **+** au cinéma / au centre-ville / en France **+** avec ma famille / avec mes amis. – Last year / Last week **+** I went **+** to the cinema / to the town centre / to France **+** with my family / with my friends.

Note: Make sure to write *je suis allée...* if you're a girl! (If you're a boy, it is just *je suis allé...*) For the reason why, go to the bottom of pg. 90.

3) J'ai rencontré **+ noun** – I met **+ noun**

   i) J'ai rencontré un tas de **filles** qui étaient bien faites. – I met loads of hot **girls**.

   ii) J'ai rencontré un tas de **mecs** qui étaient bien faits. – I met loads of hot **guys**.

Tip: Never use *rencontrer **avec***. In French, you do **not** *meet **with*** someone, you just *meet* someone.

4) J'ai passé beaucoup de temps à **+ inf.** – I spent a lot of time **+ pr.p.**

   J'ai passé beaucoup de temps à **me détendre** avec un livre. – I spent a lot of time **relaxing** with a book.

Note: *un* livre – a book   *une* livre – a pound

Imperfect

1) Quand j'étais plus jeune, **+ imperfect** – When I was younger, I used to **+ inf.**

   Quand j'étais plus jeune, **je jouais** au foot tous les samedis, mais maintenant je dois passer beaucoup de temps à faire mes devoirs. – When I was younger, I used **to play** football every Saturday, but now I have to spend a lot of time doing my homework.

2) Il faisait beau. – The weather was nice.

3) J'étais en train de **+ inf.**.... quand **+ passé composé** – I was in the process of **+ pr.p.**.... when **+ perfect**

   J'étais en train de **nager** dans la mer quand un requin m'**a mordu(e)**. – I was in the process of **swimming** in the sea when a shark **bit** me.

4) J'étais sur le point de **+ inf.**....quand **+ passé composé** – I was just about to **+ inf.**.... when **+ perfect**

   J'étais sur le point d'**aller** au centre-ville quand **il a commencé** à pleuvoir. – I was just about **to go** into town when **it started** to rain.

5) Il fallait que **+ subj.** – It was necessary that **+ verb**

   Il fallait que **j'aille** à Londres parce que je voulais acheter de nouveaux vêtements et les magasins y sont fantastiques. – It was necessary that I **go** / I needed to go to London because I wanted to buy some new clothes and the shops there are fantastic.

General Past

1) Après avoir / être / m'être **+ pa.p.** – Having **+ pa.p.**

Note: See pg. 90 for when to use *avoir* or *être* as this applies when using both the above expression and the second expression in this list. Also remember that when using *être*, the past participle must agree with whatever or whoever did the action. (Put an '*e*' on the end if feminine, an '*s*' on the end if plural or '*es*' if feminine and plural.)

Après être **arrivés** au centre-ville, nous sommes allé**s** au restaurant. – Having **arrived** at the shopping centre, we went to a restaurant.

2) Ayant / Étant / M'étant **+ pa.p.** – Having **+ pa.p.**

Ayant **mangé**, j'ai décidé de regarder la télé parce que j'étais très fatigué(e). – Having **eaten**, I decided to watch TV because I was very tired.

3) Avant de **+ inf.** – Before **+ pr.p.**

Avant d'**aller** au centre commercial, nous avons décidé de prendre quelque chose à manger. – Before **going** to the shopping centre, we decided to have something to eat.

4) Je venais de **+ inf.** – I had just **+ pa.p.**

Je venais de **quitter** la maison quand je me suis rendu compte que j'avais oublié mes clefs. – I had just **left** the house when I realised that I had forgotten my keys.

5) J'aurais aimé **+ inf.** – I would have liked to have **+ pa.p.**

J'aurais aimé **sortir** avec Jean-Claude, mais je devais aider ma mère en travaillant dans le jardin. – I would have liked to have **gone out** with Jean-Claude, but I had to help my mum by working in the garden.

6) Je me suis rendu compte du fait que j'avais raison / tort. – I realised that I was right / wrong.

7) Si j'avais / j'étais / je m'étais **+ pa.p.**..., j'aurais / je serais / je me serais **+ pa.p.**... – If I had **+ pa.p.**..., I would have **+ pa.p.**...

Note: Again see pg. 90 for when to use *avoir* or *être* as this applies when using the above expression. If using *être*, the past participle must agree.

i) Si j'avais **su** que Sam était en Espagne, j'y serais **allé(e)** aussi. – If I had **known** that Sam was in Spain, I would have **gone** there as well.

ii) Si j'étais **allé(e)** au centre-ville, j'aurais **acheté** un cadeau pour ma sœur. – If I had **gone** to the town centre, I would have **bought** a present for my sister.

Future

1) Je vais **+ inf.** – I am going to **+ inf.**

Ce week-end je vais **faire** mes devoirs. – This weekend I am going **to do** my homework.

2) J'ai l'intention de **+ inf.** – I intend to **+ inf.**

J'ai l'intention d'**aller** aux Etats-Unis avec ma famille pendant les grandes vacances. – I intend **to go** to the U.S.A. with my family during the summer holidays.

3) Quand **+ future** – When **+ present**

Note: ...I know that this is not really a phrase, but it is important to remember that when using '*when*' to signify a future event (e.g. *when I'm 18...*) in French, you have to use '*quand* + future'. So you can't just say '*quand j'ai 18 ans*', you have to say '*quand j'aurai 18 ans*'.

4) J'espère que... – I hope that...

(3 & 4) Quand **j'irai** au Portugal, j'espère qu'il ne fera pas trop chaud. – When **I go** to Portugal, I hope that it's not too hot.

<u>Conditional</u>

1) J'aimerais **+ inf.** – I would like to **+ inf.**

   Quand j'aurai dix-sept ans, j'aimerais **apprendre** à conduire. – When I'm seventeen, I would like **to learn** to drive.

2) Je dirais que... – I would say that...

   Je dirais qu'on ne peut pas visiter l'Angleterre sans aller à Londres. – I would say that you can't visit England without going to London.

3) Si j'avais beaucoup de **+ noun**, **+ cond.** – If I had lots of **+ noun**, **+ cond.**

   Si j'avais beaucoup d'**argent**, **je passerais** mes vacances dans un hôtel cinq étoiles. – If I had lots of **money**, **I would spend** my holidays in a five-star hotel.

4) Je préfèrerais **+ inf.** – I would prefer to **+ inf.**

   J'aime être grand(e) mais je préfèrerais **être** petit(e). – I like being tall but I would prefer **to be** small.

5) On pourrait... – You (in general) could...

   On pourrait protéger l'environnement en recyclant. – You could protect the environment by recycling.

6) On devrait... – You (in general) should...

   On devrait éviter de manger trop de sel. – You should avoid eating too much salt.

Opinion Phrases

Present Opinions

1) Je pense qu'il est vraiment **+ adj.** de **+ inf.** – I think that is very **+ adj.** to **+ inf.**

   Je pense qu'il est vraiment **important** de **rester** en forme parce qu'il y a trop d'obésité de nos jours. – I think that it is very **important to stay** fit because there is too much obesity nowadays.

2) Je ne pense pas que **+ subj.** – I don't think that **+ verb**

   Malheureusement, je ne pense pas que mon frère **puisse** venir avec nous au Japon, parce qu'il va en Ecosse avec sa copine. – Unfortunately, I don't think that my brother **can** come with us to Japan because he is going to Scotland with his girlfriend.

3) Je le / la trouve **+ adj.** – I find him / her / it **+ adj.**

Note: Use *Je trouve ça* **+ adj.** to mean *I find it* **+ adj.** when talking about a concept or the act of doing something, rather than a specific noun. For an example of this, look at the second paragraph of the sample essay on pg. 50.

   Je ne m'entends pas bien avec George car je le trouve **intolérable** quand il parle de ses exploits. – I don't get on well with George because I find him **intolerable** when he talks about his achievements.

4) À mon avis, c'est **+ adj.** que **+ subj.** – In my opinion, it's **+ adj.** that **+ verb**

   À mon avis, c'est **excellent** que mon frère **fasse** tant de choses pour protéger l'environnement. – In my opinion, it's **excellent** that my brother **does** so much to protect the environment.

5) Pas étonnant que **+ subj.** – No wonder **+ verb**

   Pas étonnant qu'**il fasse** chaud ici, il n'y a pas de climatisation. – No wonder **it's** hot in here, there's no air conditioning.

Past Opinions

1) Ce qui m'a plu le plus, c'était de pouvoir **+ inf.**... parce que... – What I enjoyed the most was being able to **+ inf.**... because...

   Ce qui m'a plu le plus, c'était de pouvoir **faire la fête** tous les soirs parce que j'aime bien passer du temps avec mes amis. – What I enjoyed the most was being able **to party** every night because I love spending time with my friends.

2) J'ai toujours rêvé de **+ inf.** – I have always dreamt of **+ pr.p.**

   Je voudrais aller à Paris parce que j'ai toujours rêvé d'y **aller** avec ma copine / mon copain. – I would like to go to Paris because I've always dreamt of **going** there with my girlfriend / my boyfriend.

3) i) Je l'ai trouvé(e) **+ adj.** – I found him / her / it **+ adj.**
   ii) Je l'ai trouvé(e) si **+ adj.** que… – I found him / her / it so **+ adj.** that…

Note: Ensure you add an 'e' to the end of *trouvé* if the thing you are talking about is a feminine noun (as illustrated in the examples below). Also, use *J'ai trouvé ça* **+ adj.** to mean *I found it* **+ adj.** when talking about a concept or the act of doing something, rather than a specific noun. For an example of this, look at the second paragraph of the sample essay on pg. 50.

   i) (Feminine) Je pense que la toile que j'ai vue hier était vraiment belle. Je l'ai trouvée **stupéfiante**. – I think that the painting that I saw yesterday was really beautiful. I found it **stunning**.

   ii) (Masculine) Le foot était excellent. Je l'ai trouvé si **passionnant** que je veux revenir au stade le week-end prochain. – The football was excellent. I found it so **exciting** that I want to go back to the stadium next weekend.

4) Ça m'a beaucoup plu. – I really enjoyed it. (*literally: It pleased me a lot.*)

5) C'était une expérience que je n'oublierai jamais. – It was an experience I'll never forget.

6) i) Je me suis bien amusé(e). – I had a great time.
   ii) Nous nous sommes bien amusé(e)**s**. – We had a great time.

List of useful...

The lists below contain the most common verbs in the French language. You must know and be able to recognize **all** of these in the infinitive form as well as in the basic tenses if you want to give yourself any chance of success.

Infinitives

acheter – to buy
adorer – to love
aimer – to like
aller – to go
avoir – to have
conduire – to drive
devoir **+ inf.** – to need/have to **+ inf.**
donner – to give
écouter – to listen
faire – to do/make
finir – to finish
habiter – to live
jouer – to play
lire – to read
manger – to eat
mettre – to put
nager – to swim
parler – to speak
partir de – to leave/go out from
penser – to think
préférer – to prefer
prendre – to take
pouvoir **+ inf.** – to be able to **+ inf.**
rester – to stay
travailler – to work
vouloir **+ inf.** – to want to **+ inf.**
voir – to see

Past Participles

acheté – bought
adoré – loved
aimé – liked
allé* – gone
eu – had
conduit – driven
dû **+ inf.** – needed/had to **+ inf.**
donné – given
écouté – listened
fait – done/made
fini – finished
habité – lived
joué – played
lu – read
mangé – eaten
mis – put
nagé – swum
parlé – spoken
parti* de – left/gone out from
pensé – thought
préféré – preferred
pris – taken
pu **+ inf.** – been able to **+ inf.**
resté* – stayed
travaillé – worked
voulu **+ inf.** – wanted to **+ inf.**
vu – seen

Present Participles

allant – going
ayant – having
conduisant – driving
étant – being
faisant – doing/making
jouant – playing
travaillant – working

Conditionals
All in 1st person singular *(I)* form

j'aimerais – I would like
j'aurais – I would have
j'irais – I would go
je préférerais – I would prefer

Subjunctives
All in 1st person singular *(I)* form

je fasse – I do/make
je puisse – I am able to **+ inf.**
je veuille – I want to **+ inf.**
j'aie – I have
j'aille – I go
je voie – I see

* Must agree because this verb 'takes' *être* in the compound tenses (see pg. 90).

Adjectives

Remember that all these adjectives (and any you look up) are given in the masculine singular form. If you use them in an essay, ensure you make them agree with the noun they are describing - including yourself if you're a girl - in both gender (masculine / feminine) and number (singular / plural).

Feelings, Emotions & Opinions

amusant – fun
content – happy / satisfied
déprimé – depressed
fatigué – tired
malade – ill

ravi – really happy
relaxant – relaxing
sain – healthy
triste – sad

Overused Opinions

Some adjectives used to express opinion are overused and unimpressive to examiners. Sometimes, a particular word (even if it's a bit unimpressive) has to be used in order to get across the intended meaning. However, if another makes sense, replace the more boring word with one of these:

intéressant – interesting
attirant – appealing
captivant – captivating
charmant – charming
pédagogique – educational
impressionnant – impressive

mauvais / mal – bad
affreux – dreadful
dégoûtant – disgusting
effrayant – appalling
nul – rubbish
pourri – rotten

bon – good
sensationnel – sensational
fabuleux – fabulous
fantastique – fantastic
excellent – excellent
génial – awesome
étonnant – astonishing
super – brilliant

ennuyeux – boring
assommant – deadly boring
agaçant – annoying

Connecting Words

The following table is full of incredibly useful connecting words to help you create the long sentences required in order to achieve the highest **Use of language** mark. They will also allow you to link from one sentence to the next.

Connecting Words	Meaning	Example
parce que / car	because	J'aimerais visiter Paris **parce que / car** j'ai entendu dire qu'il y a un tas de restaurants d'excellente qualité.
mais	but	Je voudrais rester chez toi **mais** je ne peux pas.
donc	therefore / so	Le professeur était assommant, et **donc** sa classe n'apprenait rien.
ensuite / puis / plus tard	then / next / later	Je suis allé(e) au cinéma, **ensuite / puis / plus tard** au centre-ville.
quand	when	**Quand** j'aurai dix-sept ans, j'obtiendrai mon permis de conduire.
de plus / en plus / en outre / d'ailleurs	furthermore / moreover / also	Elle est très intelligente et sympathique. **De plus / En plus / En outre / D'ailleurs**, elle joue du piano et de la guitare.
cependant / toutefois	however	On peut nager dans la piscine à tout moment. **Cependant / Toutefois**, c'est interdit de nager dans la mer.

puisque	since / seeing that	**Puisque** l'inspecteur est parti, je peux me relaxer.
malgré cela	despite that	Ma sœur me prend la tête. **Malgré cela** je dois nettoyer la maison avec elle.
d'abord	first (of all) / firstly	**D'abord**, nous sommes allés au restaurant.
néanmoins	nevertheless	Cette préparation est difficile, **néanmoins** elle est nécessaire.
tout en (+present participle)	while	Elle courait **tout en** mangeant un biscuit.
quant à	as for	Il pense qu'elle a raison. **Quant à** moi, je ne suis pas du tout d'accord.
tandis que	whereas	Mon père prend son thé sucré, **tandis que** ma mère le préfère sans sucre.

Note: Sorry to keep banging on about this but it is so important: *parce que* and *car* should be used regularly throughout your essays because you should be giving:

- Justifications for why you did things
- What you thought of the things you did
- Why you have that opinion

Tip: Avoid using the connectors *aussi* and *alors* because these two words have different uses to the words *also* and *so* in English. If you use them, the chances are you will do so incorrectly. Instead, use *de plus / en plus* etc. and *donc* respectively. For more information on *aussi*, go to pg. 103.

Time Expressions

Here is a list of 10 basic time expressions. You should always use these in essays and oral conversations to show the examiner whether you are talking about the past, present or future.

1) il y a trois mois... – three months ago...
2) la semaine dernière... – last week
3) le week-end dernier... – last weekend...
4) l'été dernier... – last summer...
5) de nos jours... – nowadays...
6) maintenant... – now...
7) l'année prochaine... – next year...
8) quand j'aurai dix-huit ans... – when I'm 18...
9) ce week-end... – this weekend...
10) pendant... – during...

More Time Expressions

At the moment		In the past	
avant-hier	the day before yesterday	**l'avant-veille**	two days before
hier	yesterday	**la veille**	the day before
aujourd'hui	today	**ce jour-là**	(on) that day
demain	tomorrow	**le lendemain**	(on) the next day
après-demain	the day after tomorrow	**le surlendemain**	two days later

Negatives

ne... pas – not
ne... plus – no longer
ne... rien – nothing
ne... jamais – never

ne... personne – nobody
ne... que – only
ne... ni... ni – neither... nor

Sample Essay Question

Here is a sample essay on holidays, packed full of great expressions. (The French is on the left and the English translation is on the right.) The task / title is as follows:

You recently travelled to France on holiday. Write about your visit, including:

- *What you normally do for your holidays*
- *How you travelled to France*
- *What you saw and did as well as your opinion of French food*
- *Where you will go on future holidays and why*

[1]**Normalement** je passe deux semaines avec mes amis dans le sud-est de l'Espagne [5]**parce que** les vols ne sont pas trop chers et [4]**je pense que** les plages sont très belles. [6]**Bien que** [8]**je doive** dépenser beaucoup d'argent, [4]**à mon avis** les vacances avec mes amis sont amusantes [5]**car** je peux sortir en boîte de nuit avec eux et [7]**donc** [6]**je me sens** libre!

[2]**L'été dernier**, je suis allé(e) en France avec ma famille et nous avons passé des vacances [6]**pleines d'activités**. Nous y sommes allés en voiture et [4]**j'ai trouvé ça** assez ennuyeux mais [4]**j'ai beaucoup aimé** voir la belle campagne.

[7]**Quand** il faisait beau, nous sommes allés à la plage et [4]**ce que j'ai aimé le plus, c'était de pouvoir** nager dans la mer [5]**parce que** l'eau n'était pas trop chaude et [6]**il faisait trente degrés**. [4]**Ça me fait plaisir de** nager [5]**parce que** c'est excellent pour la santé et [4]**je crois que** c'est agréable. [7]**De plus**, [6]**j'ai passé beaucoup de temps à** prendre un bain de soleil [5]**car** [6]**j'ai**

I [1]**normally** spend two weeks with my friends in the south-east of Spain [5]**because** the flights aren't too expensive and [4]**I think that** the beaches are beautiful. [6]**Although** [8]**I have to** spend lots of money, [4]**in my opinion** holidays with my friends are fun [5]**because** I can go out clubbing with them and [7]**therefore** [6]**I feel** free!

[2]**Last summer**, I went to France with my family and we had a holiday [6]**full of activities**. We went by car and [4]**I found that** quite boring but [4]**I really liked** looking at the beautiful countryside.

[7]**When** it was sunny, we went to the beach and [4]**what I enjoyed most was being able** to swim in the sea [5]**because** the water was fresh and [6]**it was thirty degrees**. [4]**I love** swimming [5]**because** it's excellent for my health and [4]**I think that** it's enjoyable. [7]**Also**, [6]**I spent a lot of time** sunbathing [5]**because** [6]**I've**

toujours rêvé d'avoir la peau bronzée. [7]En outre, [4]j'ai beaucoup aimé me détendre avec un livre d'Harry Potter, [7]et donc j'en ai lu trois.

[2]Le lendemain, j'ai rencontré [6]une fille bien faite / [6]un garçon bien fait qui m'a préparé un repas typique de la région et [4]je pense que [6]c'était une expérience que je n'oublierai jamais. J'ai pris des champignons grillés et ils étaient [4]magnifiques!

[3]L'année prochaine, [6]j'ai l'intention d'aller au Portugal avec mes amis. [4]Malheureusement, je ne pense pas que mon meilleur ami [8]puisse venir avec nous. [6]J'espère qu'il fera beau et [4]j'aimerais rencontrer une autre fille charmante / un autre garçon charmant. [6]Quand j'aurai dix-huit ans, j'irai aux Etats-Unis [5]parce que [6]je dois dire que la culture là-bas m'intéresse beaucoup et [4]je voudrais voir un match de football américain.

always dreamt of having tanned skin. [7]Furthermore, [4]I really liked relaxing with a Harry Potter book, [7]and so I read three of them.

[2]The next day, I met [6]a good-looking girl / [6]a good looking boy, who prepared me a typical meal from the region and [4]I think that [6]it was an experience that I'll never forget. I had grilled mushrooms and they were [4]magnificent!

[3]Next year, [6]I'm planning on going to Portugal with my friends. [4]Unfortunately, I don't think that my best friend [8]can come with us. [6]I hope that the weather is nice and [4]I would like to meet another charming girl / another charming boy. [6]When I'm eighteen, I'll go to the U.S.A. [5]because [6]I must say that the culture over there interests me greatly and [4]I would love to see an American football game.

[1]- Time expression ('I normally') shows you are answering the 1st bullet point in the present.
[2]- Time expressions show you are answering the 2nd & 3rd bullet points in the past.
[3]- Time expression shows you are answering the 5th bullet point in the future / conditional.
[4]- Opinion phrase
[5]- Reason in order to explain why you have an opinion about something
[6]- Very natural 'standard' French phrase
[7]- Connecting word
[8]- Subjunctive... **MARKS!!**

Notice that throughout this sample essay, the spread of different colours is fairly even with:

- A mixture of standard phrases, opinion phrases and reasons for these opinions
- Plenty of connecting words and time expressions
- A few subjunctives to really boost the **Use of language** mark

When you write essays, the key is to manipulate phrases to suit the essay title, just as I have done in this sample essay. Looking at the sample essay again, with the mark scheme (which gives marks for: **Communication**, **Use of language** and **Accuracy**) in mind, we can see that:

1. There are 5 paragraphs in response to the 4 bullet points (I split one bullet point into two parts). Tenses are used correctly throughout each paragraph. Each paragraph responds specifically to each part of the essay title. The essay is easy to understand and makes sense. Therefore, it will be awarded **full marks** for **Communication**.
2. There are plenty of constructions, all correctly used, which add fluidity to the essay. A few subjunctives are also thrown in! So, **full marks** for **Use of language**.
3. There are no spelling mistakes and there are no mistakes in the use of tenses. All verbs agree with their subjects (the thing doing the verb) and all adjectives agree with their nouns. (This was made easier by using the checking rule, which comes soon on pg. 54.) Therefore, it would be given **full marks** for **Accuracy**. Please be aware that, although there are no mistakes in this essay, you will be allowed to make some relatively small mistakes and still be awarded full - or close to full - marks for **Accuracy** in your exam. You are not expected to be perfect!

… Finally, I would like to emphasise the point I made right at the start of this guide: You do **not** (in reality) have to have done everything you write about in your essay. You will probably have noticed, in my sample essay, that I wrote about going on holiday with my friends and liking this because I can go clubbing with them. I can say for a fact that I have never been on holiday with friends and gone out clubbing because, aside from the fact I am nowhere near that cool, it's also illegal! The reason I included that sentence was to make you realise and remember that your essay absolutely does not have to be factually correct… You **must** make it up to show off your use of French!

Sentence Structure Formula

You hopefully remember that in order to boost your mark for **Use of language** you need to use longer sentences. This is true... **BUT** do not make them more than a few lines long or you will begin to make mistakes and they will become confusing.

So, what you need to do is: try to use a combination of phrases (often a standard phrase with an opinion phrase) in order to produce more complex sentences. You can then link these phrases and sentences together with time expressions and connecting words.

Here is an example of how this works:

Present phrase	**Normalement, je passe trois semaines en Espagne**
parce que	**parce que**
Opinion phrase	**je pense qu'il est très important de me détendre**
Time expression	**de nos jours**
Connecting word	**et donc**
Time expression	**l'année dernière**
Past phrase	**j'ai décidé d'aller à Toulon**
Opinion phrase	**et j'ai trouvé ça très relaxant.**

Clearly, the above structure is not a hard-and-fast structure which you have to use for every single sentence you write; evidently that would be ridiculous. However, it ought to give you an example of how you can string together plenty of the different structures I have shown you. I can tell you with absolute certainty that doing so correctly will greatly boost your mark in any (I)GCSE essay or oral examination. Using this idea, you ought to get into the habit of giving reasons for virtually everything you say by using a mixture of standard phrases, opinion phrases and the words *parce que* or *car*.

The Checking Rules

You now know how to boost your mark for **Communication** and **Use of language**, but how can you improve your **Accuracy** mark?

I am afraid, unless you want to spend hours learning vocabulary lists, I cannot help you with your spelling. However, there is an essay checking formula which, once you have written an essay, should be used without exception (as long as you have time). It is in **2 parts**:

PART 1:

- Have your completed essay in front of you and take out a pencil.
- Underline, in pencil, each verb (word of doing) (e.g. *il parle - he speaks*)... Make sure you don't miss one out!
- Now, go back to the top of the essay, to the first underlined verb.
- Ask yourself four questions about this verb:
    - What is the verb supposed to say in English (e.g. *he speaks*)?
    - What tense is the verb in, in English (e.g. *he speaks* is present)?
    - What person (I, you (sg.), he / she / it, we, you (pl.), they) is that verb, in English? (e.g. *he*)
    - What is the infinitive (i.e. the '*to*' form of the verb) in English, then in French? (e.g. *to speak - parler*)
- Now you need to check the ending of the verb using your knowledge of verb conjugation. Make sure you are comparing it with the correct tense of the correct type of verb (-*er*, -*ir* or -*re*).

Tip: If there are two parts of verbs next to one another (e.g. *Je **suis allé(e)***) and the first part is a part of *avoir* or *être* (e.g. **suis**), the second part must be a past participle (e.g. ***allé(e)***). If the first part is not part of *avoir* or *être*, the second part must be an infinitive (e.g. *Elle **peut sortir***).

- Rub out the pencil under this verb and correct it if you were wrong.
- Repeat the process on every verb.

Note: For more explanation on the use of different tenses and how to construct them, have a look at the *Verbs* section which starts on pg. 76.

PART 2:

- Having completed Part 1, go back to the start of your essay (don't worry, this won't take as long as Part 1) and underline, in pencil, every adjective (descriptive word) (e.g. *fantastique* - *fantastic*) and carry out the following procedure on every word now underlined:

- Make sure that the adjective you are using is correctly positioned with respect to the noun it describes. (Does that adjective go before or after the noun?) Adjectives which go before the noun can be found on pg. 93.

- Ask yourself: "What noun is this adjective describing?" (e.g. *une femme* or *un homme*)
  - Is that noun masculine or feminine? (If you don't know whether a noun is masculine or feminine, just make an informed guess. Have a look at *The Rules of Sex* section on pg. 96 for help on working this out.)
  - Is the noun singular or plural? (Is there one or more than one?)

- Using your answers to the questions above, apply the following rule which works for the **vast majority** of French adjectives:

  - If the noun is masculine and singular, the adjective does not change from the form in which it is given in a dictionary.
  - If the noun is masculine and plural, an '*s*' should have been added to the end of the adjective.
  - If the noun is feminine and singular, an '*e*' should have been added to the end of the adjective.
  - If the noun is feminine and plural, '*es*' should have been added to the end of the adjective.

  … However, like all things in languages, there are some irregulars which don't quite follow this pattern. If you want to learn some of these, go to pg. 97 or look up '*irregular French adjectives*' online or in a grammar book!

- Correct any mistakes you may have made in the agreement of that adjective and rub out the pencil mark under that word.

Points to Remember for the Writing Exam

- You can make up anything you want, as long as you know how to say it and it is relevant to the essay title

- Write a paragraph per bullet point or per part of the essay title (depending on the form in which the task / title is given to you)

- Use different tenses: *passé composé*, imperfect, present, future & conditional (at least!)

- Use both standard phrases and opinion phrases as much as possible (without forcing them)

- Give reasons for why you like(d) / dislike(d) something

- Use time expressions and connecting words to link ideas and write longer sentences (but not too long!)

- The Checking Rules

> YOU MAY NOT HAVE TO DO THIS. If your teacher has not told you about preparing a picture for your oral presentation, skip this page!

Oral Picture Presentation

If you have to describe a photo in your oral examination (as your presentation), here are some phrases for describing a picture:

- Ma mère a pris cette photo-là quand... – My mum took this photo when...
- L'année dernière... – Last year
- Pendant un séjour scolaire – During a school trip
- Comme on peut voir sur l'image... – As you can see in the photo...
- Cette scène s'est déroulée... – The scene took place...
- Avec plusieurs membres de ma famille – With several members of my family
- Quand nous avons loué un appartement en France – When we rented an appartment in France
- À gauche, on voit mon frère... – On the left, we see my brother...

Position words to describe a photo:

- à gauche – on the left
- à droite – on the right
- à côté de – next to
- près de – near to
- au premier plan – in the foreground
- à l'arrière plan – in the background

Oral Exam Questions by Topic Area

Here is a list of virtually every question you could be asked in your (I)GCSE examination. The questions are split up into different oral topic areas. If you are doing a standard GCSE, you should only prepare questions which are related to your task(s). However, for IGCSE, you may be asked any of these questions and so should prepare answers for most of them (**if they are on your syllabus**).

Topic Area I – Personal Relationships

Tu peux te décrire physiquement?
Quelle sorte de personnalité as-tu?
Parle-moi de ta famille.
Quels sont les avantages / inconvénients d'avoir des frères ou des sœurs?
Tu t'entends bien avec ta famille?
Qu'est-ce qui provoque des disputes entre toi et tes parents?
Pourquoi les adultes trouvent-ils difficile de comprendre les jeunes?
La famille est-elle importante pour toi?
Parle-moi de ton meilleur ami.
Que faites-vous ensemble?
Tu te disputes parfois avec tes amis? Pourquoi?
Quelle est l'importance des amis?
Quelles sont les qualités d'un copain / d'une copine idéal(e)?
Qu'est-ce que tu as fait avec tes amis le week-end dernier?
Quels sont les problèmes les plus importants dans ta vie?

Topic Area II – Holidays & Tourism

Tu aimes voyager? Pourquoi?
Tu as déjà visité un autre pays? Lequel?
Qu'est-ce que tu as fait? C'était bien?
Qu'est-ce que tu as pensé de la nourriture?
Où préfères-tu passer les vacances?
Tu préfères rester dans un camping ou à l'hôtel?
Quels pays étrangers voudrais-tu visiter?
Tu préfères l'Angleterre ou l'étranger pour les vacances? Pourquoi?
Tu es déjà allé(e) en France? Raconte-moi…
Quelles sont les différences entre la vie en France et en Angleterre?
Comment passeras-tu les vacances d'été cette année?
Parle-moi de tes vacances idéales.

Topic Area III – Your Area & The Modern World

Tu habites dans une ville ou un village?
Parle-moi un peu de ta ville / ton village.
Est-ce qu'il y a des distractions pour les jeunes?
Qu'est-ce qu'il y a d'intéressant à faire dans ta région?
Qu'est-ce qu'il y a pour les touristes dans ta région?
Quels sont les problèmes dans ta région?

Tu t'intéresses au problème de l'environnement? Pourquoi?
Qu'est-ce que tu fais pour protéger l'environnement?
Est-ce que tu fais quelque chose pour aider l'environnement à l'école?
À ton avis, quel est le problème le plus important pour l'environnement?
Que devrait faire le gouvernement?
Qu'est-ce qu'il va se passer si on ne fait rien?
Est-ce que tu penses que le réchauffement de la terre posera des problèmes à l'avenir dans ton pays? Lesquels?

Les actualités / nouvelles sont-elles importantes pour toi? Pourquoi?
Qu'est-ce qui se passe dans ton pays en ce moment?
Que penses-tu de la publicité?
As-tu un téléphone portable? Est-ce que tu penses que les jeunes sont devenus obsédés par leurs portables?
Quels sont les avantages des téléphones portables? Et les inconvénients?
Est-ce que tu penses que les ordinateurs sont utiles?
Quelle sera la place des ordinateurs à l'avenir?
Tu utilises beaucoup Internet?

Topic Area IV – Leisure

Quels sont tes passe-temps préférés?
Tu es sportif / sportive?
C'est important de faire du sport?
Quels personnages sportifs admires-tu en particulier? Pourquoi?
Qu'est-ce que tu as fait le week-end dernier?
Que feras-tu ce soir?
Qu'est-ce que tu vas faire le week-end prochain?
Qu'est-ce que tu as fait pendant les vacances de Pâques?
Tu joues d'un instrument de musique?
Qu'est-ce que tu aimes comme musique?
Préfères-tu écouter des CDs ou assister à un concert? Pourquoi?
Pourquoi la musique est-elle importante pour toi?

Quelle sorte de films aimes-tu?
Quel film as-tu vu récemment?
Quel est ton film préféré?
Quel(le) est ton acteur / actrice préféré(e)?
Tu regardes souvent la télé?
Quelle est ton émission préférée?
Quels sont les avantages / dangers de la télévision?
Est-ce que tu penses que les jeunes regardent trop de télévision?

Topic Area V – Home Life

Où habites-tu?
Décris-moi ta maison / ton appartement.
Décris-moi ta chambre.
Qu'est-ce que tu fais dans ta chambre?
Qu'est-ce que tu fais pour aider à la maison?
Qu'est-ce que tu détestes faire?
Qui fait la cuisine chez toi?
Comment serait ta maison idéale?
Raconte-moi une journée typique.
Qu'est-ce que tu as mangé pour tes repas hier?
Qu'est-ce que tu aimes manger pour le petit-déjeuner?
Qu'est-ce que tu vas manger ce soir?
Quel est ton plat préféré?
Est-ce que tu as un régime sain?
Etre végétarien, qu'est-ce que tu en penses?
Quels conseils me donnerais-tu pour que je reste en bonne santé?
Tu es en forme?
Tu fais beaucoup de sport?
Comment pourrait-on encourager les gens à faire plus de sport?
Les régimes sont-ils dangereux?
Est-ce que tu fumes? Pourquoi?
Pourquoi est-ce que certains jeunes commencent à fumer?
Comment peut-on décourager les jeunes de fumer?
Est-ce que tu bois de l'alcool? Pourquoi?
Quels sont les dangers de la drogue?

Topic Area VI – School & Work Life

Parle-moi de ton collège.
Quelles matières est-ce que tu étudies au collège?
Quelle est ta matière préférée? Pourquoi?
Est-ce qu'il y a une matière que tu n'aimes pas du tout?
Quels sont les avantages / inconvénients de ton collège?
Combien de cours as-tu par jour?
Que fais-tu pendant la récréation?
Tu manges à la cantine? Qu'est-ce que tu penses de la nourriture?
Décris-moi une journée typique au collège.
Tu portes un uniforme? Qu'est-ce que tu en penses?
Quels sports fais-tu au collège?
Il y a de bonnes installations sportives?
Il y a des activités parascolaires à ton collège?
À ton avis, est-ce que tu reçois une bonne éducation?
Comment est-ce qu'on pourrait améliorer ton collège?
Qu'est-ce que tu as l'intention d'étudier au mois de septembre?
Tu iras à l'université? Pourquoi?
Quelle carrière voudrais-tu suivre?
Comment est-ce que tu gagnes ton argent de poche?
Tu as un petit boulot?
Tu as déjà fait un stage en entreprise? C'était une expérience positive?
Où seras-tu en 2030?

Section III

Specific Essential Learning

Vocabulary

There are a few condensed vocab lists starting on pg. 65. These contain words which are likely to come up in the reading and listening papers, particularly in the first few sections. You must learn these lists thoroughly as all of this vocab is certainly expected of you at (I)GCSE. (However, this is not a guarantee that it will definitely come up!) It is also important that you realise that these lists are nowhere near exhaustive and that you must do your own vocab learning if you want to succeed in your French exams.

There is some essential vocab which you simply cannot do without (obviously you aren't going to understand anything without some core knowledge of the basics.) There are tonnes of fairly extensive vocab lists online or in GCSE vocab books. Regardless of which vocab lists you choose to use, I would advise you to go through the most important sections (such as topics you are likely to want to write an essay on or speak about in your oral), highlighting vocab you don't know. Then, follow my three Golden Rules for learning vocabulary:

GOLDEN RULE :
LEARN IT IN SMALL CHUNKS, BUT REGULARLY

I would advise learning 4-7 words only, but learning them daily. Have a list of words which you want to learn on a sheet (print off a GCSE vocab list from your exam board for example) and highlight all the ones you are not 100% certain of on one day. (This might take a bit of time - why not go and do it now?) Then, each day for around 10 minutes - perhaps while eating breakfast or before going to bed - learn 4-7 of those words (you decide exactly how many). Test yourself, and once you can remember the English translation of each French word, you're done for the day.

GOLDEN RULE :
COME UP WITH WAYS OF REMEMBERING WORDS

It's hard to just learn stuff which has no significance to you, for example a random list of words. Therefore, I use little sayings, which are really weird (**BUT** they work for me) to help me remember vocab. For example, *un routard* is *a backpacker*, I remember this: 'Always take a roulade with you when you go backpacking', because *routard* sounds like *roulade*!

GOLDEN RULE :
REVISE VOCAB

Learning vocab can be incredibly dull, but it is vital. It is easy to become frustrated when you have learnt 5 words one day and then, within 3 days, have forgotten them completely. So, in the first Golden Rule, I said to learn 4-7 words a day, but this would mean you forgot the vast majority of the vocab within a week. Therefore, every 4 or 5 days, don't learn anything new. Instead, spend 10 minutes testing yourself on the vocab you have been learning over the past few days. Then, any words which you have forgotten (there will probably be a few) should be underlined and re-learnt as if they were new to you (as one of your 4-7 daily words).

All this might sound complicated, but it really isn't. Just spend a few minutes every day doing it and it will automatically become part of your routine. Just think how much you will learn from such a small amount of time every day: within a year you will have learnt at least 600 words.

Basic Vocab

Les Sports et Les Passe-temps – Sports and Hobbies

aller à la pêche	to fish
athlétisme (m)	athletics
basket (m) , basket-ball (m)	basketball
cheval (m)	horse
faire du cheval, monter à cheval, faire de l'équitation	to ride (horse)
équitation (f)	horse riding
cyclisme (m) , vélo (m)	cycling
danse (f)	dancing
danser	to dance
échecs (m pl)	chess
escalade (f)	climbing
faire de la voile	to sail
foot (m) , football (m)	football
jouer , pratiquer	to play, to perform
nager	to swim
natation (f)	swimming
patin à glace (m)	ice skating
ski (m)	skiing
ski nautique (m)	water skiing
tennis (m)	tennis
tennis de table (m) , ping-pong (m)	table tennis
tir à l'arc (m)	archery
voilier (m)	sailing boat

Note: You cannot say *jouer au sport* to mean *to play sport*. In English it is acceptable to say *play sport*, but in French this is grammatically incorrect. Therefore, you must say *to do sport*, so it's *faire du sport*.

L'Apparence et La Personnalité – Appearance and Personality

L'Apparence (f)	Appearance
beau / belle	pretty
blanc	white
bronzé	dark-skinned , tanned
cheveux (m pl)	hair
cheveux roux (m pl)	ginger hair
court	short
fort	strong
grand	tall
gros / grosse	fat
laid, moche	ugly
long / longue	long
maigre	thin
marron (never agrees!)	chestnut
noir	black
obèse	obese
peau (f)	skin
petit	small
tache de rousseur (f)	freckle

La Personnalité	Personality
aimable , gentil / gentille , sympa	kind , pleasant
amusant , drôle , marrant	funny
égoïste	selfish
fier / fière	proud
intelligent	intelligent
méchant	naughty , nasty
paresseux	lazy
timide	shy
triste	sad

Le Temps et Les Saisons – Weather and Seasons

Le Temps	Weather
beau (temps)	good weather
brumeux	foggy
bulletin météo (m)	weather report
chaleur (f)	heat
ciel (m)	sky
degré (m)	degree (temperature)
éclair (m) , foudre (f)	lightning
froid	cold
mauvais (temps)	bad weather
neige (f)	snow
il neige	it is snowing
nuage (m)	cloud
nuageux	cloudy
orage (m)	storm
pluie (f)	rain
il pleut	it is raining
pluvieux	rainy
sec	dry
soleil (m)	sun
vent (m)	wind
venteux	windy

Note: To say *it is* followed by some sort of weather (e.g. *it is sunny*) you say *il fait* **NOT** *il est*. Similarly, to say *it was* (e.g. *it was windy*) you must use *il faisait* **NOT** *il était*. Also, notice that you use the imperfect here, **NOT** the *passé composé*. So, you never say: *il a fait beau*, but instead say: *il faisait beau*.

Les Saisons (f pl)	Seasons
(en) automne (m)	(in) autumn
(**au**) printemps (m)	(in) spring
(en) été (m)	(in) summer
(en) hiver (m)	(in) winter

Les Vêtements et La Mode – Clothes and Fashion

Les Vêtements (m pl)	Clothes
baskets (f pl)	trainers
chapeau (m)	hat
chaussette (f)	sock
chaussure (f)	shoe
chemise (f)	shirt
ceinture (m)	belt
costume (m)	suit
cravate (f)	tie
écharpe (f)	scarf
gant (m)	glove
jupe (f)	skirt
maillot de bain (m)	swimming costume
manteau (m)	coat
montre (f)	watch
pantalon (m) **(sg NOT pl)**	trousers
parapluie (m)	umbrella
portefeuille (m)	wallet
porte-monnaie (m)	purse
pull (m)	sweater , jumper
sac à main (m)	handbag
survêtement (m)	tracksuit
tee-shirt (m)	T-shirt

La Mode	Fashion
à pois	spotted
à rayures , rayé	stripy
en coton	made of cotton
en cuir	made of leather
en laine	made of wool
en soie	made of silk

Les Matières – Subjects

allemand (m)	German
anglais (m)	English
biologie (f)	biology
chimie (f)	chemistry
théâtre (m)	drama
dessin (m)	art
EPS (éducation physique et sportive) (f)	PE
espagnol (m)	Spanish
français (m)	French
géographie (f)	geography
histoire (f)	history
informatique (f)	ICT
langues étrangères (f pl)	foreign languages
maths (f pl)	maths
physique (f)	physics
science (f) / sciences naturelles (f pl)	science / biology
éducation religieuse (f)	religious studies
technologie (f)	DT

Le Transport – Transport

à pied	on foot
(en) avion (m)	(by) plane
(en) bateau (m)	(by) boat
billet (m)	ticket
conduire	drive
embouteillage (m)	traffic jam
(en) moto (f)	(by) motorbike
(en) train (m)	(by) train
(en) voiture (m)	(by) car

La Nourriture – Food (Difficult ones only!)

Les Fruits (m pl)	Fruit
ananas (m)	pineapple
cerise (f)	cherry
citron (m)	lemon
fraise (f)	strawberry
framboise (f)	raspberry
pamplemousse (m)	grapefruit
pêche (f)	peach
poire (f)	pear
pomme (f)	apple
raisin (m)	grape

Les Légumes (m pl)	Vegetables
chou (m)	cabbage
chou-fleur (m)	cauliflower
concombre (m)	cucumber
haricots verts (m pl)	green beans
petits pois (m pl)	peas
pomme de terre (f)	potato

Généralement	Generally
frites (f pl)	chips
fruits de mer (m pl)	seafood
glace (f)	ice cream
jambon (m)	ham
œuf (m)	egg
pâtes (f pl)	pasta
poisson (m)	fish
poulet (m)	chicken
soupe (f) , potage (m)	soup
viande (f)	meat

Les Emplois – Jobs

agent de police (m)	police officer
boucher (m)	butcher
boulanger (m)	baker
chauffeur (m)	driver
coiffeur (m) / coiffeuse (f)	hairdresser
directeur (m) / directrice (f)	headteacher , manager
homme au foyer (m) / mère au foyer (f) *or* femme au foyer (f)	house husband / house wife
facteur (m)	postman
fermier (m) / fermière (f)	farmer
infirmier (m) / infirmière (f)	nurse
ingénieur (m)	engineer
médecin (m) , docteur (m)	doctor
professeur (m) , prof (m)	teacher
secrétaire (f)	secretary
serveur (m) / serveuse (f)	waiter / waitress
vendeur (m) / vendeuse (f)	shop assistant
vétérinaire (m)	vet

Note: In French, you do **NOT** use *un* or *une* before the name of a job. For example:

- Ma mère est coiffeuse. – My mum is a hairdresser.
- Je vais devenir médecin à l'avenir. – I am going to become a doctor in the future.

L'Environnement – The Environment

améliorer	to improve
arbre (m)	tree
augmenter	to increase
boîte (f)	tin (can)
bouteille en verre (f)	glass bottle
bruyant	noisy
carton (m)	cardboard
champ (m)	field
circulation (f)	traffic
cultiver	to grow
déboisement (m)	deforestation
déchets (m pl)	waste
économiser	to save
effet de serre (m)	greenhouse effect
emballage (m)	packaging
espace vert (m)	green space
gaspiller	to waste
gaz d'échappement (m pl)	exhaust fumes
incendie (m)	fire
nettoyer	to clean
piste cyclable (f)	cycle lane
pollué	polluted
poubelle (f)	bin
propre	clean
quartier (m)	district , area
sac **en** plastique (m)	plastic bag
sale	dirty
transports en commun (m pl) , transports publics (m pl)	public transport
usine (f)	factory
zone piétonne (f)	pedestrian zone

Faux Amis

These French words are similar to words in English, but actually mean something entirely different from their lookalikes. **Examiners love these!**

actuel / actuelle	current , present
actuellement	currently , at the moment
addition (f)	bill
adresse (f)	skill (*can be address too*)
affaire (f)	business , matter
appréciation (f)	assessment
assister à	attend , to be present at
attendre	to wait for
avertissement (m)	warning
blesser	to wound
car (m)	coach (*also* because)
cave (f)	cellar
chair (f)	flesh
chance (f)	luck
chips (f pl)	crisps
coin (m)	corner
costume (m)	suit (*can be costume too*)
crayon (m)	pencil
déception (f)	disappointment
décevoir	to disappoint
déguster	to taste
demander	to ask for
dent (f)	tooth
essence (f)	petrol
étiquette (f)	ticket , label
éventuellement	possibly , might , may
fabrique (f)	factory
formation (f)	training (*can be formation too*)
formidable	great , terrific , fantastic
four (m)	oven

génial	brilliant
gentil	kind , nice , likeable
histoire (f)	story (*can be history too*)
hôtel de ville (m)	town hall
journal (m)	newspaper
journée (f)	day
lecture (f)	reading (*activity or matter*)
librairie (f)	bookshop
location (f)	renting , letting
magasin (m)	shop
médecin (m)	doctor
monnaie (f)	change (*coins*) , currency
nouvelle (f)	piece of news , short story
passer un examen	to take an exam
pathétique	moving
pièce (f)	room
plaisanterie (f)	joke
préservatif (m)	condom
promenade (f)	walk , stroll
prune (f)	plum
prétendre	to claim
quitter	to leave
raisin (m)	grape
réaliser	to create , undertake
rentable	profitable
reporter	to postpone
rester	to stay
sensible	sensitive
stage (m)	(training) course
sympathique	nice , pleasant
travail (m)	work
vacances (f pl)	holiday , holidays
veste (f)	jacket , coat

Cutting Out Grammar Errors

When you write in French, you need to turn yourself into a computer which follows a series of steps to produce a word-by-word, grammatically correct sentence. Do this over and over again and you will have a number of grammatically correct sentences which form a grammatically correct essay. Simple.

The biggest hindrance to this is forgetfulness. Because we are used to talking in English without thinking about grammar, we naturally write in French in a similar way. You translate words from English to French in your head, and then write them down to form sentences. We have to override this natural flow of words to make our minds focus on the grammar involved. We must concentrate on each word to ensure we do not forget to make things grammatically correct. The sections which follow aim to give you the ability to cut out grammar errors... You just have to make sure you remember to follow the rules.

> **GOLDEN RULE :**
> **DON'T FORGET GRAMMAR**

Ohhh... and one more thing you have heard a couple of times before:

> **GOLDEN RULE :**
> **WRITE WHAT YOU KNOW, DON'T WRITE WHAT YOU**
> **DON'T KNOW**

Verbs

When studying languages, all students tend to hate verbs! They are the most important part of any language in order to boost your grade grammatically because the simple fact is: knowing how to use verbs instantly makes you stand out as a strong candidate. In reality, they are very straightforward. You merely need to know:

- Which tense to use
- How to form each tense according to:
  - Which tense you are using
  - Which person you are using from:

Person	French	English	Example
1st Person Singular	*je/j'*	*I*	*I want an ice-cream.*
2nd Person Singular	*tu*	*you* (singular)	*You have a car.*
3rd Person Singular	*il* **or** *elle* **or** *on** **or** *a name*	*he* **or** *she* **or** *it* **or** *you (in general)** **or** *a name*	*Sally ate all the pies.*
1st Person Plural	*nous* **or** *1 or more names et moi*	*we* **or** *1 or more names and I*	*Tim and I have no friends.*
2nd Person Plural	*vous*	*you* (plural) **or** *you (polite form)*	*You two have lots of money.*
3rd Person Plural	*ils* **or** *elles* **or** *2 or more names*	*they* **or** *2 or more names*	*Joan, Tom and Pete are vets.*

*See pg. 101 to find out more about the usage of *on*

Note: If there were two girls involved in an action, you would use *elles*, but as soon as there is a male involved you must use *ils*. So if Jack, Lucy, Jane and Sally were doing something, you would still use *ils* (even though there are more girls than boys; I'm sorry it's sexist!)

So, I am going to take you through what each tense means and when each tense should be used. Then we shall look, precisely and in a very easy-to-understand way, at how you can ensure you don't make any grammar errors using each tense, and therefore boost your grade.

What each tense means

First of all, let's look at what each tense is used for in French along with examples (in English) of when it would be used.

Tenses	To...
Present	1) Say what you **normally** do.
	2) Say what you are **currently** doing.
	E.g.1 *I **eat** fish all the time.*
	E.g.2 *I **am** looking for a boyfriend.*
Imperfect	1) Give a general description in the past (normally of a feeling or an opinion).
	2) Describe what you **used** to do.
	3) Describe something that **was** happening **when** suddenly something else happened (imperfect + perfect).
	E.g.1 *He **felt** happy because it **was** exciting.*
	E.g.2 *I **used to** ride all the time.*
	E.g.3 *I **was** watching TV **when** my mum came in.*

Passé composé (Perfect)	1. Describe a completed action in the past. This is always used for something that someone did but has now stopped. 2. Say I **have** never / always... E.g.1 *"Last night I only **drank** one beer, Mum!"* E.g.2 *I **have** always dreamt of going to Miami, but I **have** never liked flying.*
Pluperfect	Often describe something longer ago in the past than the perfect tense. It is used whenever in English you say I **had** + past participle. E.g. *Once I **had** finished eating, I went to town.*
Future (with *aller*)	Say what you **are going** to do in the immediate future. E.g. *Next week, I **am going** to buy a car.*
Futur Simple (Future)	Say what you **will** do in the more distant future. E.g. *I **will** go to Las Vegas when I'm 21.*
Future Perfect	Say what you will have done in the future when (by the time) something else happens. E.g. *I **will have** eaten all the cake by the time mum gets back.*
Conditional	Portray something theoretical. It is used in English whenever you say I **would**... E.g. *I **would** try skydiving but I am too scared.*
Conditional Perfect	Portray something theoretical in the past. It is used in English whenever you say I **would have** + past participle. E.g. *I **would have** liked to have done it when I was younger, but now I am too old.*

Getting Rid of Verb Errors

The table we have just seen is probably a fairly scary one. There are 9 tenses included... "That is all far too difficult when you can barely work out how to use the present tense" is what many school teachers would tell you. This is a load of rubbish! In fact, the present and imperfect tenses are by far the hardest tenses to use and form, and if you have even the slightest grasp of these, using the other tenses really is easier. Trust me; the supposedly more difficult and complex tenses towards the end of the previous table - which will gain you **LOADS OF MARKS** - really are simple to form.

So, let's go through each tense and work out how to boost your grammar mark by using each correctly.

Present Tense

Like I just said, the present tense is difficult. This is because there are so many irregulars and unfortunately the irregulars tend to be the most commonly used verbs.

You need to know how to form regular present tense verbs. If you don't, ask your teacher and make sure you learn it! The irregulars are harder to learn... Ideally, you would know every part of every irregular verb in every tense, but this is pretty unrealistic and actually unnecessary to achieve a top grade. What I would advise you do is learn the 1st person singular, 3rd person singular and 1st person plural (if you don't know what these mean have a look at pg. 76) of 5 of the most common irregulars, and then make sure you use these in your essays. I do not include *avoir* and *être* in that list because these need to be learnt fully and we will see why in a minute!

Verb	1st Person Singular	3rd Person Singular (*elle* or *on* or a *name* can replace *il*)	1st Person Plural (*1 or more names et moi* can replace *nous*)
aller (to go)	je vais	il va	nous allons
venir (to come)	je viens	il vient	nous venons
faire (to do/make)	je fais	il fait	nous faisons
prendre (to take)	je prends	il prend	nous prenons
dire (to say)	je dis	il dit	nous disons

So, those verbs are crucial to learn and use in your essays. There are also two golden saviours for you to employ when you are not certain of a verb's formation in the person you want to use. The first saviour is to use a present tense phrase (found on pg. 36), many of which simply require you to know the infinitive of the verb you want to use. The second saviours are verbs which are followed by an infinitive. The best ones to use are shown on the next page.

	pouvoir (to be able to)	devoir (to have to)	vouloir (to want to)	aimer (to like)
je/j'	peux	dois	veux	aime
tu	peux	dois	veux	aimes
il/elle/on	peut	doit	veut	aime
nous	pouvons	devons	voulons	aimons
vous	pouvez	devez	voulez	aimez
ils/elles	peuvent	doivent	veulent	aiment

So, if I wanted to say: *I go to the beach every weekend*, but couldn't remember the parts of *aller* (which I should know!), I'd instead say: *I like to go to the beach every weekend*.

*Je **vais** à la plage tous les week-ends.* – I go to the beach every weekend.

*J'aime **aller** à la plage tous les week-ends.* – I like to go to the beach every weekend.

Note: In English, *weekend* is one word. In French, it is hyphenated to *le week-end*. It is also quite unusual in that it is pronounced in the same way in French as it is in English.

Similarly, if I wanted to say: *they do sport each Sunday*, but hadn't learnt the 3rd person plural (*they*) form of the verb *faire*, I could instead say: *they are able to do sport each Sunday*.

*Ils **font** du sport chaque dimanche.* – They do sport each Sunday.

*Ils **peuvent** faire du sport chaque dimanche.* – They are able to do sport each Sunday.

Imperfect Tense

The imperfect has no irregulars. Its stem is always formed by taking the *nous* form of the present tense and adding the following endings:

Pronoun	Ending
je/j'	-ais
tu	-ais
il/elle/on	-ait
nous	-ions
vous	-iez
ils/elles	-aient

Of course, the problem is knowing the *nous* form of the present tense if the verb is irregular. So, I would advise you to stick to either regular verbs, or the 5 verbs we just looked at, or *avoir* and *être* which I will come onto in a minute.

The hardest thing about the imperfect is knowing when to use it. If you want to show off your knowledge of forming and using it, the four easiest ways to do so are:

1. Use *c'était* meaning *it was* (from *être*) along with an adjective to demonstrate your opinion of something.
2. Use *il y avait* meaning *there was* or *there were*. (For more on *il y a* constructions have a look at pg. 105.)
3. Have something which was happening (in the imperfect), when something else happened (in the *passé composé*).
4. Describe the weather in the past using *il faisait...* E.g. *Il faisait beau, donc nous avons décidé d'aller au parc.*

Futur Simple & Conditional Tenses

These two tenses are formed in a very similar and easy way. Unfortunately, there are irregulars to learn. However, they aren't too difficult as the only part that is irregular is the stem; the endings are always the same. Another positive is that you already know the conditional endings because they are exactly the same as the imperfect ones (which we have just covered). Even better, the future endings are very similar to the present parts of *avoir*, which you have to know anyway. So, you need to know the stem of the future and conditional. For regulars, it is shown below. Then you simply have to add the imperfect endings to form the conditional and the endings at the bottom of the page for the future:

Infinitive Ending	Remove	Add	Example
-er	Nothing!	Nothing!	*composer* has stem *composer-*
-ir	Nothing!	Nothing!	*finir* has stem *finir-*
-re	e	Nothing!	*vendre* has stem *vendr-*

Pronoun	Endings
je/j'	-ai
tu	-as
il/elle/on	-a
nous	-ons
vous	-ez
ils/elles	-ont

Here are the most common irregular verbs in the future and conditional tenses:

Verb	Stem	1ˢᵗ Person Singular Future	1ˢᵗ Person Singular Conditional
aller **(to go)**	*ir-*	j'irai	j'irais
devoir **(to have to)**	*devr-*	je devrai	je devrais
faire **(to do/make)**	fer-	je ferai	je ferais
pouvoir **(to be able to)**	*pourr-*	je pourrai	je pourrais
venir **(to come)**	viendr-	je viendrai	je viendrais
voir **(to see)**	verr-	je verrai	je verrais
vouloir **(to want to)**	*voudr-*	je voudrai	je voudrais

Future Tense (with *aller*)

This is extremely easy to form and is comparable to saying *I am going to...* in English. You simply use the pronoun or noun, the correct part of the present tense of *aller* and an infinitive.

Pronoun or **Noun** + **Part of *aller*** + **Infinitive**

E.g. Je vais aller en ville. Mon père va venir avec moi. Nous allons faire du shopping.

This is a great way to use the future, particularly in an oral, if you forget an irregular future stem, or just panic and forget a future ending. However, be wary! Examiners will want to see the *futur simple*, which we have just covered, in your essay or to hear it during your oral. Using that will get you more marks than using the future with *aller*.

> **Tip:** The *futur simple* and the future with *aller* are used pretty much interchangeably in French, just like saying *I will* and *I'm going to* in English. They have slightly different meanings, so in English it sounds slightly unnatural to say: *I will leave this Tuesday*. Instead, you'd say: *I'm going to leave this Tuesday*. However, you certainly will not be marked down for using one instead of the other in terms of their meaning... But, bear in mind what I have just said about needing to use the *futur simple*.

Passé Composé, Pluperfect, Future Perfect & Conditional Perfect

Now we are coming towards what are generally considered the 'very difficult' and 'advanced' tenses. However, these four tenses are all formed in a very similar way. Rather than having a pronoun or a noun and one other word, these have a pronoun or a noun and two other words:

Pronoun or **Noun** + **Part of** *avoir* or **Part of** *être* + **Past Participle**

E.g.   **Tim**   **a**   **mangé**

To form these four compound tenses, you simply need to use a different tense of *avoir* or *être* (and we have already covered each of these four tenses)! So, which tense of *avoir* or *être* do you need to use for each compound tense?

Compound Tense	Tense of *avoir* or *être*
Passé Composé	Present
Pluperfect	Imperfect
Future Perfect	Future
Conditional Perfect	Conditional

Therefore, the two most important verbs for you to succeed in French are *avoir* and *être*. You need to know **all six parts** of **both** of them in the **present, imperfect, future** and **conditional** like you know how to spell your name (hopefully!). These are so important.

> **GOLDEN RULE :**
> **LEARN *AVOIR* & *ÊTRE***

avoir

	present	imperfect	future	conditional
j'	ai	avais	aurai	aurais
tu	as	avais	auras	aurais
il/elle/on	a	avait	aura	aurait
nous	avons	avions	aurons	aurions
vous	avez	aviez	aurez	auriez
ils/elles	ont	avaient	auront	auraient

être

	present	imperfect	future	conditional
je/j'	suis	étais	serai	serais
tu	es	étais	seras	serais
il/elle/on	est	était	sera	serait
nous	sommes	étions	serons	serions
vous	êtes	étiez	serez	seriez
ils/elles	sont	étaient	seront	seraient

So, now we have the pronoun or noun and the part of *avoir* or part of *être* sorted, what about the past participle? Back on pg. 86, we saw the example: *Tim a mangé.* If we look at this sentence grammatically, *mangé* is a past participle. In English, most past participles end in −*ed* or −*en*. E.g. played (*joué*), finished (*fini*), driven (*conduit*), eaten (*mangé*). However, there are plenty of irregulars. E.g. done (*fait*), put (*mis*), gone (*allé*). Fortunately for you, past participles are used in French in exactly the same way as in English. Slightly less fortunately, there are quite a few irregulars you need to learn!

How to form a Past Participle

For the majority of verbs in French, the past participle is formed by:

Infinitive Ending	Remove	Add	Example
-er	er	é	*composer* has past participle *composé*
-ir	r	Nothing!	*finir* has past participle *fini*
-re	re	u	*vendre* has past participle *vendu*

Irregulars

Verb	Past Participle
avoir (to have)	eu
boire (to drink)	bu
courir (to run)	couru
devoir (to have to)	dû
dire (to say)	dit
être (to be)	été
faire (to do/make)	fait
lire (to read)	lu
pouvoir (to be able to)	pu
prendre (to take)	pris
recevoir (to receive)	reçu
savoir (to know how to)	su
venir (to come)	venu
voir (to see)	vu
vouloir (to want to)	voulu

Avoir or *Être*?

In French, as we have just seen, the *passé composé*, pluperfect, future perfect and perfect conditional are formed of two parts. In these cases, we must use either *avoir* or *être* and a past participle. So which do you use? *Avoir* or *être*?

There are 13 verbs - which you have to learn - which take *être* when using these four tenses and also when using either of the constructions *après avoir / être* + past participle (e.g. *après être allé(e)(s)* – having gone) and *ayant / étant* + past participle. All other verbs take *avoir* in these tenses and constructions.

Now when I say 'take *être*', what does this mean? This means that whenever any of the above tenses or constructions is used, the part before the past participle must be a part of *être* (never *avoir*). These thirteen verbs are all verbs of coming and going and are relatively easy to remember by the acronym:

Mrs Van de Tramp

M	monter	to go up	je suis monté(e)
R	rester	to stay	je suis resté(e)
S	sortir	to go out	je suis sorti(e)
V	venir	to come	je suis venu(e)
A	aller	to go	je suis allé(e)
N	naître	to be born	je suis né(e)
D	descendre	to go down	je suis descendu(e)
E	entrer	to enter	je suis entré(e)
T	tomber	to fall	je suis tombé(e)
R	retourner	to return	je suis retourné(e)
A	arriver	to arrive	je suis arrivé(e)
M	mourir	to die	je suis mort(e)
P	partir	to leave	je suis parti(e)

Note: *rentrer*, *revenir* and *devenir* also take *être* as they are compounds of (i.e. contain within them) *entrer* and *venir*.

You will notice by all of the past participles in the right hand column there is an extra *e* in brackets. This is because, if the thing or person doing the verb is feminine, you must add an extra *e* to the past participle. This is only the case when the verb takes *être*. Similarly, if more than one thing or person is doing the verb you must add an *s* to the past participle. If it is feminine and plural you must add *es*.

Examples of the *Passé Composé*, Pluperfect, Future Perfect & Conditional Perfect

Just to give you an idea of how you might use these tenses in an essay, here are some sample sentences.

> **Note:** There are also some phrases starting on pg. 38 containing all of these tenses, but I'm hoping once you understand the grammar, you will be able to make your own ones up too.

Passé Composé: **J'ai** toujours **aimé** faire de la natation et, par conséquent, **je suis allé(e)** à la piscine avec ma sœur et **nous avons nagé** pendant une heure. – I have always liked swimming and so I went to the pool with my sister and we swam for an hour.

Pluperfect: Pas étonnant que je ne me sois pas senti bien; **J'avais mangé** deux poulets, **j'avais bu** trois pintes de bière et **j'avais** peu **dormi**. – No wonder I felt ill; I had eaten two chickens, I had drunk three pints of beer and I had barely slept.

Future Perfect: À l'âge de trente ans, **j'aurai acheté** une grande maison. – When I am thirty, I will have bought a big house.

Conditional Perfect: **J'aurais lu** cinq livres et **j'aurais couru** tous les jours si j'étais allé(e) en vacances. – **I would have read** five books and **I would have run** every day if I had gone on holiday.

Reflexives

Reflexive verbs are a type of verb we do not have in English. When a tense is formed of two parts (as seen previously) in the *passé composé*, pluperfect, future perfect or conditional perfect, reflexive verbs always take *être*. Therefore, they follow the agreement rules (adding *e*, *s* or *es*) covered on pg. 90.

> **Note:** Verbs only agree when you are using one of the compound tenses and when the verb is either reflexive or one of those thirteen verbs which takes *être*. So, for example, a present tense reflexive **doesn't** agree.

So what are reflexive verbs? They are verbs which involve someone doing something to himself / herself. So, for example, in French *je me lève* translates literally to *I get myself up*. There are quite a few reflexive verbs and they are mostly to do with your daily routine. They behave in the same way as ordinary verbs like the ones we have been looking at, except that you have to add in an extra 'part' when you form reflexive verbs. It is immediately after the pronoun or noun doing the verb and needs to agree with this pronoun / noun. So...

Pronoun or **Noun** + **Extra Part** + **Main Part of Verb** = **Fully Formed Reflexive**

So what is this extra part?

Pronoun / Noun	Extra Part
je	me/m'
tu	te/t'
il/elle/on	se/s'
nous	nous
vous	vous
ils/elles	se/s'

Adjectives

Adjectives are words which describe nouns. In French, unlike in English, they nearly always go after the noun they describe. So, in English we say *the strong boy*, in French you must say *the boy strong*, which translates to *le garçon fort*.

Adjectives that go Before the Noun

There are a few exceptions to this. These are all common adjectives, so learn that they must go **before** the noun in order to avoid seeming like a lower standard candidate.

beau	bon	gentil	joli	mauvais
méchant (nasty)	vilain (ugly)	grand	gros	haut
vaste	jeune	nouveau	vieux	
petit		premier		deuxième

*E.g. Ma **petite** sœur va être une **jolie** femme.*

Agreement

To boost your grade, the most crucial aspect to understand concerning adjectives is agreement. So many students seem to panic when they hear that 'dreaded' word. This really is not difficult... It is far easier than what we have just covered in the *Verbs* section. Essentially, when you learn adjectives, they are given in the masculine singular form. If a noun is feminine or plural or both, you need to change this form. For most adjectives, simply:

- Add an **e** if the noun it describes is **feminine singular**
  - La fille fort**e**
- Add an **s** if the noun it describes is **masculine plural**
  - Les garçons fort**s**
- Add **es** if the noun it describes is **feminine plural**
  - Les filles fort**es**

There are, like all things in languages, irregulars. If you get the occasional irregular adjective wrong, you **will not** be heavily penalised. If you make mistakes with basic regular agreement you **will** be penalised. However, if you really want to shine as a top-level candidate, getting irregular agreement right is a good way to do it. Here are a few irregulars you can use pretty easily in an essay which will boost your grade by showing off your grammar knowledge:

English	Masculine Singular	Before Vowel	Feminine Singular	Masculine Plural	Feminine Plural
expensive	cher	cher	chère	chers	chères
happy	heureux	heureux	heureuse	heureux	heureuses
beautiful	beau	bel	belle	beaux	belles
new	nouveau	nouvel	nouvelle	nouveaux	nouvelles
old	vieux	vieil	vieille	vieux	vieilles

Often, people don't drop marks in their exams because they don't know how to make regular adjectives agree, but because they forget to make them agree. This is because we don't do it in English. So, look at the checking rules for every time you write in French; the second rule on pg. 55 applies to making sure adjectives agree. However, first and foremost, make sure you remember the Golden Rule and don't forget grammar!

Nouns

All you really need to be able to do concerning nouns in French to boost your grade is tell what gender (masculine or feminine) a noun is and be able to put it into the plural. You need to be able to tell the gender of a noun so that you use the correct version of *the* (i.e. *le*, *la*, *l'* or *les*) and also so that you can make any adjective that may accompany that noun agree (as we have just seen).

The first thing to note is that if you are given a noun in a reading comprehension or an essay title, do not then use it in an answer or an essay in the wrong gender. This just shows you are careless and gives an examiner completely the wrong impression. There was an example of this in a mock paper I did, in which 8 out of 24 people who took the mock did the following:

Question: Qu'est-ce qu'on peut observer dans **une** image au musée?

Response: Dans **un** image on peut observer…

So, a third of my class were incapable of copying the gender of *image* correctly on the line below the question. This is madness and will probably lose you a mark!

GOLDEN RULE :
DON'T GET NOUN GENDERS WRONG IF YOU ARE GIVEN THEM

So, aside from that, you need to try and learn the genders of words as part of your vocab learning, but in reality it is not as important as learning the words themselves and can be pretty difficult to remember. So, here is a dummy's guide to working out the gender of a word which will work the vast majority of the time.

The Rules of Sex

There are always exceptions, and I will give you a few of them if they are important for you to know... If they are pretty rare words, I'm not going to waste your time saying you should learn them because there are more important things to be concentrating on. To start with, if a noun ends in an *e* it will be feminine 90% of the time. However, this is occasionally overridden by a few of the following noun endings which are always masculine:

Note: The ones in bold are most important!

Ending	Example(s)	Exception(s)
-acle	un miracle	
-age	le fromage	une image, la plage, la page, la rage, la nage, la cage
-al	un cheval	
-amme	un programme	
-eau	un oiseau	
-ème	le système, un problème	
-er	le boulanger	**la mer**
-et	un béret	
-isme	le tourisme	
-ment	le commencement	
-oir	le miroir	

There are also a few noun endings which are always feminine, even though they do not end in an *e*:

Ending	Example	Exception(s)
-sion	la télévision	
-tié	la moitié	
-té	la santé	
-tion	la notation	

Plural Nouns

So, how do you make a noun plural?

Just as with adjectives, you put an *s* on the end of the noun. There are a few exceptions to this and they simply have to be learnt. These exceptions are nouns with particular endings which sometimes require a change of ending to make them plural; you cannot simply always add an *s*.

Singular Ending	Plural Ending	Singular Example	Plural Example
-al	-aux **or** -als	animal bal	animaux bals
-ail	-aux **or** -ails	travail détail	travaux détails
-eau -eu	add *x*	chapeau lieu	chapeaux lieux
-s -x -z	No change	corps voix gaz	corps voix gaz

Tips and Tricks – Golden Nuggets to Remember

Nugget	Example
Vacances The word *vacances* (holiday(s)) is never singular. In French, you must say *I went on holidays* **NOT** *I went on holiday.* It is also feminine.	Je suis allé(e) en vacances l'année dernière. **NOT** Je suis allé(e) en vacance l'année dernière.
Beaucoup de / d' It's always *beaucoup de* (a lot of) **OR** *beaucoup d'* if followed by a vowel. Never: *beaucoup du* **OR** *beaucoup de la* **OR** *beaucoup des* **OR** *beaucoup + anything else*! Note that *beaucoup de / d'* is often followed by a plural noun, but still does not change.	J'ai mangé beaucoup de chocolat. **NOT** J'ai mangé beaucoup du chocolat. Il y a beaucoup de choses à faire. – There are lots of things to do.
Countries When you say *in* or *to* a country, you use: *en* + feminine country *au* + masculine country *aux* + plural country The majority of countries in French are **feminine**. If you are saying you went on holiday somewhere, use a country which you have already learnt the gender of. I would choose one country from each gender and one plural one. Then, always use these countries in your essays because it is good to show you know about how to use the genders of countries correctly.	Feminine: Il est allé en **France**. Nous sommes en **Chine**. (*China*) Je voudrais aller en **Afrique du Sud**. (*South Africa*) Je veux rester en **Angleterre**. (*England*) Masculine: J'aimerais aller au **Canada**. J'irai au **Mexique** l'année prochaine. Je suis au **Zimbabwe**. Plural: Je suis allé(e) aux **Etats-Unis**.

Le week-end

In French, *the weekend* has a hyphen. So it is *le week-end*.

Tous les **week-ends** je vais chez mon père.

Chez

chez + a person means *at / to the person's house*

Je suis chez Hugo. – I'm at Hugo's house.

Je suis allé(e) chez Nathan. – I went to Nathan's.

Préférer

You do not say *préférer **de** + infinitive*. There is no *de*, so the correct phrase is *préférer + infinitive*.

J'aime sortir avec Jules, mais je préfère sortir avec Léo.

Qui or Que ?

If, **IN ENGLISH**, the verb comes immediately after the word *who*, use *qui*.

If, **IN ENGLISH**, something else comes after the word *who*, use *que*.

In English: I saw my friend **who works** (*who + verb*) hard.

In French: J'ai vu mon ami **qui** travaille dur.

In English: The man **who I** (*who + something else*) saw works hard.

In French: L'homme **que** j'ai vu travaille dur.

Do not confuse:

voir – to see
regarder – to watch

écouter – to listen
entendre – to hear

parler – to speak
dire – to say

Par exEmple

It is not *par ex**a**mple*.

J'aime bien faire du sport. Par ex**e**mple, je joue au rugby tous les lundis.

Quelque chose de / d'

To say *something* + *adjective* in French, you cannot simply say *quelque chose* + *adjective*, you must add in a *de* or *d'* if followed by a vowel and say *quelque chose de / d'* + *adjective*.

Hier, j'ai vu quelque chose **de** différent. **NOT** Hier, j'ai vu quelque chose différent.

Demain je ferai quelque chose **d'**intéressant. **NOT** Demain, je ferai quelque chose intéressant.

Faire du sport

It's always *faire du sport*, never *jouer au sport* in French. In English, we can sort of say *play sport* (although it sounds a bit weird), but in French it is a big *No!*

However, note that you can say *je joue au rugby*... So you can play a specific sport, just not sport in general.

Je fais du sport tous les jours après avoir fini au lycée. **NOT Je joue au sport** tous les jours après avoir fini au lycée.

Make sure you use apostrophes

... Pretty much whenever there is:

- a word with 3 letters or less
- ending in *e*
- next to another vowel or a silent *h*.

Or when there are two *i* letters next to one another.

The most common errors in forgetting to do this are with:

que + il = qu'il **NOT** *que il*
que + elle = qu'elle **NOT** *que elle*
que + on = qu'on **NOT** *que on*

And with:

si + il = s'il **NOT** *si il*

BUT:

si + elle = si elle **NOT** *s'elle*
si + on = si on **NOT** *s'on*

Basic:

- **j'**aime faire du sport
- **c'**était fantastique
- je **l'**adore

Most common errors:

(Notice that lots of the apostrophes are correct, but these sentences are ruined by one silly mistake.)

- Je l'aime parce **que elle** est jolie.
- Je pense **que il** est très sympa.
- J'arriverai en retard **si il** neige.
- L'homme m'a dit **que on** peut faire du ski en France.

Time

So many people make mistakes when trying to say they did something at a specific time in French. So, to avoid this, always use the following method:

à + *hours* h *minutes* (with the hours using the 24 hour system).

Je suis arrivé(e) à 11h30.

Hier, elle s'est endormie à 22h30.

Partir and *Quitter*

In French, there are two ways of saying *to leave* (*to go away from*):

- partir
- quitter

Often people make mistakes when using these. Firstly, *partir* takes être in compound tenses (see pg. 90), while *quitter* does not. Secondly, and the most common error, *partir* must be followed by *du / de la / des / de l'* while *quitter* is followed by *le / la / les / l'*.

Je vais partir **de la** maison à 11h00.

Elle est partie **du** magasin il y a une heure.

Je vais quitter la maison à 11h00.

Elle a quitté le magasin il y a une heure.

On

This little word is underused by (I)GCSE students. As you become more familiar with French you realise that it is used very often. It literally translates to *one*, but this is outdated in English and no one (other than maybe the Queen) says *one has seen some splendid sport this summer*! We would instead say *we have seen...*

So, it is used virtually interchangeably in French with *nous* and so can mean **we**, and is always used when **generalising** about what **you** can do.

J'aime aller en Afrique du Sud parce qu'**on** peut voir beaucoup d'animaux. – I like going to South Africa because **you** can see lots of animals.

On y va – (*literally*) We go there – Let's go

Si **on** allait en Chine, **on** verrait beaucoup de pollution. – If **you** went to China, **you**'d see a lot of pollution.

Moins

This word has the potential to lose you marks because, depending on the way it is used, it can mean two entirely opposite things.

It is quite often used in reading or listening exercises to try and trick you, so watch out for it!

au moins... means *at least...*

moins de... means *less than...*

On voit qu'en France il y a **au moins** dix millions de gens qui fument. – You can see that in France there are **at least** 10,000,000 people who smoke.

On voit qu'en France il y a **moins de** dix millions de gens qui fument. – You can see that in France there are **less than** 10,000,000 people who smoke.

Tout le monde

When using *tout le monde* to mean *everyone* or when using other groups of people using *tout* or *toute* (e.g. *toute ma famille*), you must remember that this is a **singular** group of people. There may be more than one person, but there is only one group. Therefore, any verb which follows this must be in the 3rd person **singular** (*it*) **NOT plural**. Also, any adjectives which agree must be in the **singular NOT plural**.

Tout le monde **aimerait** avoir beaucoup d'argent. **NOT** Tout le monde **aimeraient** avoir beaucoup d'argent.

Toute ma famille ét**ait** content**e**. **NOT** Toute ma famille ét**aient** content**es**.

Pendant not Pour

In French, when talking about an action in the past, present or future which took / takes / will take place **for** a certain amount of time, you must use *pendant* instead of the literal translation *pour* in order to avoid ever making a mistake.

(There are times when you can use *pour*, but there are also times when it is wrong to do so. Therefore, just stick to *pendant* and you're guaranteed to be correct!)

Je suis allé(e) en France **pendant** deux semaines. **NOT** Je suis allé en France **pour** deux semaines.

Chaque semaine, je vais au parc **pendant** deux heures pour jouer au foot avec mes amis. **NOT** Chaque semaine, je vais au parc **pour** deux heures pour jouer au foot avec mes amis.

Depuis + present

In English, we say **I have been doing** something for 5 years. Therefore, students often translate this using depuis + *passé composé*... However, in French, you must use the present instead of the *passé composé*.

Je joue au golf depuis dix ans. – I have been playing golf for ten years.

If you want to really impress the examiner, maybe use the construction *ça fait X ans que* **+ present**.

Ça fait **sept** ans que **j'habite** à Londres. – I have been living in London for 7 years.

The Negative *de*

In French, when you want to say that someone doesn't have something, you always have to add in a *de* or *d'* if it is followed by a vowel.

Je n'ai pas de frères.

Il n'avait pas d'amis.

Il n'y a pas d'espace.

Aussi

The word *aussi* is normally translated as *also*. This means English people make mistakes using it, because you can place *also* pretty much anywhere in a sentence in English. This is not the case in French when using *aussi*. To make sure you don't use it incorrectly, only ever use it at the end of a sentence. Therefore, a better translation would be *as well* or *too*.

Il partira demain. Je partirai **aussi**. – He's leaving tomorrow. I'm leaving **as well**.

Je joue au squash souvent et toute ma famille joue au squash **aussi**. – I often play squash and all my family plays squash **too**.

If you want to start a sentence with *also* or *furthermore*, use the following instead of *aussi*:

- *de plus*
- *en plus*
- *en outre*
- *d'ailleurs*

J'aime regarder des films au cinéma parce que la qualité du son est meilleure que chez moi. **De plus**, l'écran est plus grand. – I like to watch films at the cinema because the quality of the sound is better than at my house. **Also**, the screen is bigger.

Do not pronounce *–ent*

Ever!!!!

Ils mangent is pronounced exactly the same as *il mange*.

Ils jouaient is pronounced exactly the same as *il jouait*.

When to pronounce a final *s*

In the oral section of your exam, a sure-fire way to sound like a lower-standard candidate is to pronounce the *s* at the end of every word. You simply sound bad! So as standard, never pronounce the *s* at the end of a word. However, if you want to sound like a really top-level candidate (which you do) there is one occasion when you should always pronounce it: when the word is followed by another word starting with a vowel.

Me**s** amis sont trè**s** importants. – My friends are very important.

Here, you pronounce the two bold letters (**s**).

Le**s** fille**s** ne veulent pa**s** rester à la plage. – The girls don't want to stay at the beach.

Here, you do not pronounce the three bold letters (**s**).

Adverbs go straight after the verb

This is a basic error that English people make all the time. (I drove my French teacher mad when I used to do this!) It is an error that is incredibly easy to avoid because the rule always applies and there are no exceptions:

When using an adverb (e.g. *beaucoup* or *bien*), the adverb always goes immediately after the first verb.

If you are using a simple tense (i.e. it is formed using a pronoun or a noun + a verb), then the adverb goes straight after the verb.

If you are using a compound tense (Future with *aller*, *Passé Composé*, Pluperfect, Future Perfect or Conditional Perfect) then the adverb goes immediately after the part of *aller*, *avoir* or *être*.

Je joue **beaucoup** au cricket. – I play cricket **a lot**.

Note: Here you can see why English people make mistakes with this. Our word order is different.

Il s'est **bien** conduit tout au long de la journée. – He behaved **well** throughout the day.

See how this works when there is a negative:

Il n'avait pas **bien** fait ses devoirs. – He hadn't done his homework very **well**.

Lots of *il y a*

In French, *il y a* means *there is* or *there are*. **It does not change in the plural.** There are lots of different forms of *il y a* that can be used in your essays to show off your knowledge of tenses.

il y a – there is / are

il y avait – there was / were (on going)

il y a eu – there was / were (completed)

il y avait eu – there had been

il y aura – there will be

il y aurait – there would be

il y aura eu – there will have been

il y aurait eu – there would have been

il doit y avoir – there must be

il devrait y avoir – there should be

il aurait dû y avoir – there should have been

il pourrait y avoir – there could be

il aurait pu y avoir – there could have been

Note: See pg. 77, 78 and 82 on when to use the imperfect or *passé composé*.

The Golden Rules

WRITING EXAM

1. Write what you know, don't write what you don't know
2. Don't write too much - there is a word limit for a reason
3. Use phrases but don't force them - if a sentence sounds unnatural, you will lose marks

ORAL EXAM

4. Say what you know, don't say what you don't know
5. Be prepared but sound spontaneous – use what you have learnt while sounding chatty
6. Expand your answers - give as much detail as possible with reasons and opinions included
7. Breathe slowly and remember: everyone is nervous before their oral!

CONTROLLED ASSESSMENTS

8. Do not use a dictionary in the exam to look up words which were not included in your prepared essay

READING & LISTENING EXAMS

9. You will not understand every word, but you don't need to
10. Know how to manipulate information in the text
11. Answer the question in the right language
12. Give the information you are asked to give

VOCABULARY

13. Learn it in small chunks, but regularly
14. Come up with ways of remembering words
15. Revise vocab

GRAMMAR

16. Don't forget grammar
17. Learn *avoir* & *être*
18. Don't get noun genders wrong if you are given them

Your Notes

Books in this Series

Follow Us Online

Discover loads of useful resources and find out about all of our current and future products by joining the Exam Grade Booster community online.

Visit us: www.examgradebooster.co.uk

Follow us: @ExamGradeBoost

Watch us: Exam Grade Booster

Like us: Exam Grade Booster

+1 us: Exam Grade Booster

Write For Us

Want to become an author yourself?	**Want to earn money?**	**Want to have something hugely impressive on your UCAS form or CV?**

Go to **www.examgradebooster.co.uk** and find the **Write for Us** page. This page should have all the information you are after, but if you have any other questions you can contact us via the website. In order to write for us, you will have to complete a very straight-forward application process (there is a short form to fill out at the bottom of the *Write for Us* page). Should you be deemed suitable to write a book, you will be given access to all of our manuscripts, formatting, cover design and branding as well as having the immediate advantage of working with people, just like yourself, who have succeeded in writing their very own books.

Do it:

- Alone
  ... It is possible; I am just like you and I have done it!
- With your friends
  ... We have a number of books being written by groups of friends to lighten the work load.

Exam Grade Booster

Lightning Source UK Ltd.
Milton Keynes UK
UKOW07f1613100516

273949UK00005B/43/P